Advance Praise for *Paschal Paradox*

Drink deeply, reader, from the well of wisdom that is Diarmuid O'Murchu. In this volume you are gifted with an overview of the history of evolutionary spirituality, how to integrate it within a Christian framework with integrity, as well as a glimpse into the author's own evolving faith over the course of a life well-lived. The paschal mystery comes alive in the lived history of a man who has successfully struggled to mine the deep and abiding mystery of what is essential about life and about the Christian faith.

—Bruce Sanguin, author, *The Way of the Wind* and *Dismantled*; psychotherapist, former minister in the United Church of Canada

Diarmuid O'Murchu has written a brave and honest book that opens our hearts and minds to the power of human reconciliation with Spirit and Earth and the necessary rebuilding of a sacred ethos for our time. *Paschal Paradox* is a tribute to one man's search for truth and the profound inner changes he undergoes to be free of punitive or exclusive cultural and religious identities, and, ultimately, to embrace a different understanding of God—an evolutionary spirituality of an expansive, unfolding universe of cosmic wonder. What makes this book particularly compelling is O'Murchu's quotidian details of soul challenges embedded in the Irish struggles, Catholic identity, and religious sectarianism.

—Beverly Lanzetta, author, *Radical Wisdom*, *The Monk Within* and *Birthing a New Mysticism;* theologian and spiritual teacher

The author's humility in moving beyond the personal narrative in every period of his life to its transpersonal consequences makes this an autobiography worth taking seriously, as his account is linked to the challenge and inspiration of his faith in God, humanity, and the entire universe. Questions and challenges this autobiography provokes us to consider are not new, but they are dealt with, with a raw honesty that should inspire and challenge every potential reader.

—Dr. Aruna Gnanadason, author, *With Courage and Compassion: Women and the Ecumenical Movement*

It feels strange to so strongly recommend this book because I feel like I am almost recommending myself, if that is not too narcissistic to say! Although Diarmuid is genuinely much more a scholar and scientist than I am, we have come to so many of the same conclusions about the Gospel, church, religious life, spirituality, and meaning itself. Read and be fed by my Irish brother.

—Fr. Richard Rohr, OFM, author, *The Universal Christ* and *The Wisdom Pattern*

Paschal Paradox

Reflections on a Life of Spiritual Evolution

Revised Edition

Diarmuid O'Murchu

ORBIS BOOKS
Maryknoll, New York 10545

Founded in 1970, Orbis Books endeavors to publish works that enlighten the mind, nourish the spirit, and challenge the conscience. The publishing arm of the Maryknoll Fathers and Brothers, Orbis seeks to explore the global dimensions of the Christian faith and mission, to invite dialogue with diverse cultures and religious traditions, and to serve the cause of reconciliation and peace. The books published reflect the views of their authors and do not represent the official position of the Maryknoll Society. To learn more about Maryknoll and Orbis Books, please visit our website at www.orbisbooks.com.

Published by Orbis Books, Box 302, Maryknoll, NY 10545-0302.

This edition is slightly amended from the original Franciscan Media edition, 2022.

Manufactured in the United States of America

Library of Congress Cataloging-in-Publication Data

Names: O'Murchu, Diarmuid author
Title: The Paschal paradox : reflections on a life of spiritual evolution / Diarmuid O'Murchu.
Description: Maryknoll, NY : Orbis Books, [2026] | Includes bibliographical references.
Identifiers: LCCN 2025051473 (print) | LCCN 2025051474 (ebook) |
ISBN 9781626986787 trade paperback | ISBN 9798888661321 epub
Subjects: LCSH: O'Murchu, Diarmuid | Catholics—Ireland | LCGFT: Autobiographies
Classification: LCC BX4705.O134 A3 2026 (print) | LCC BX4705.O134 (ebook)
LC record available at https://lccn.loc.gov/2025051473
LC ebook record available at https://lccn.loc.gov/2025051474

DEDICATION

To the memory of those who died from COVID-19, and in gratitude to the frontline workers whose sacrifice and dedication kept hope alive amid the darkness of pain and suffering.

CONTENTS

INTRODUCTION

While I thought I was learning how to live, I have been learning how to die.

—Leonardo da Vinci

This is an autobiography with a mystical twist. It is not a chronological outline from childhood through to old age. Instead I am reflecting on those times that might be described as quantum leaps in which the extraordinary infiltrated the ordinary, and from there on the territory never looked the same again. And what I had gained from the new breakthrough involved a dying and letting go of former securities. Only with hindsight did the puzzling pattern begin to make sense.

For me, it has always been a journey heavily influenced by faith. The Christian notion of dying and rising again, or, more accurately, being knocked down only to be raised up again, is a recurring theme throughout the story of my life. I describe not merely the "ups-and-downs" of life but an evolving pattern—a paschal journey—within which my personal narrative unfolds, frequently leading into the transpersonal realm in which the horizons of meaning expand and deepen.

I reflect on my life from the horizon of three score and ten years. I too have relished my youth, and I have been blessed with a long life of good health. I welcome my aging process with ambivalence and insecurity. Among my life-blessings, however, have been a series of encounters with decline and diminution that require a quality of honesty and transparency not frequently observed. Like many others I don't like those life experiences related to decline, decay, and dying.

When I look back, however, I can see that those dark times were the catalysts for some of the most creative breakthroughs in my life.

I write this for all who wrestle today with an evolutionary understanding of life, involving letting go of what at one time felt important and embracing new possibilities for growth and expansion. Nothing is stable or static anymore. Everything is in flux and moving through a multidirectional trace. None of us can escape its impact. But neither can the institutions, structures, and organizations within which we have lived and worked.

Each chapter is structured around one or more personal anecdotes of my life story (the personal), coupled with enlarged horizons of meaning that subsequently ensued (the transpersonal). While the reader is likely to be more enamored by the personal narratives, it is the transpersonal consequences that carry more meaning and significance for me. It is that same transpersonal vision that continues to challenge and inspire the meaning of my faith, in God, humanity, and indeed the entire universe.

Much of this book was written during the COVID-19 pandemic of 2020. From the beginning I had an intuitive sense that this was a paradoxical message from the Earth itself, reminding humans that if we did not change our ways we would pay a high price for our reckless manipulation of earth's resources. Several scientists have confirmed that insight, yet our governments and major institutions turn a blind eye. In this denial of death is a much more sinister denial of life's true essence and particularly the paschal journey I explore throughout this book.

At both the personal and transpersonal levels, I experience an unceasing process of birth-death-rebirth. This paradoxical dynamic is insinuated into every aspect of our contemporary world. Hopefully the landscape I am exploring will illuminate at least some of the cultural transitions of our time and, true to the spirit of the foundational Christian paschal journey, will offer hope and meaning to sustain us through the major challenges of the present and future times.

CHAPTER ONE

My Evolutionary Horizon

> *The human spirit is that moment of consciousness in which we become aware of ourselves as part of a larger whole, begin to grasp its wholeness and unity, and realize that there is a thread binding everything together and bringing a cosmos out of the chaos. By establishing a relationship with the Whole, the spirit within us turns human beings into an infinite project, wholly open to others, to the world, and to God.*
>
> —Leonardo Boff

While most biographies follow a chronological pattern from youth to old age, my life story belongs to a different rhythm. The progression is lateral rather than linear, in which adult events recapitulate experiences that belong to earlier stages, inviting thresholds of integration that often feel both exciting and frightening. There is a rhythm to my life for which the notion of *evolution* seems like a useful fit. Deep within my being, it is a construct that has nourished and sustained me across many challenging transitions.

I first came across the notion of evolution in my early twenties. It might well be the single biggest factor that made me an avid reader. Strange as it may seem now, reading scarcely featured at all in my childhood. In the impoverished conditions of my family life, the only reading material that ever entered our home was an occasional daily newspaper and free devotional magazines from our local church—both of which I rarely if ever read.

Little changed as I moved through my adolescent years. Educational literature consisted of facts and figures, much of which I learned by rote—to pass exams. My early seminary formation introduced me to scripture and spiritual reading, most of which seemed to have gone over my head. I can only assume that the greater wisdom of God also ensured that some of it lodged somewhere in the recesses of my heart.

As I shall indicate in later chapters, an intellectual awakening occurred in my early twenties—perhaps some ten years behind such development for most people—and what I can only describe as a higher (or deeper) wisdom led me into reading spiritual books that began to set my spirit on fire. Of particular significance were the writings of the priest-paleontologist Teilhard de Chardin.

The Evolutionary Imperative

Teilhard had a lot to say about evolution, the depths of which only made sense to me over several years. For the first time (I think) I began to understand the intuitive wisdom that nourished and sustained me during those years when, several years later, I read Stephen Hawking's popular work, *A Brief History of Time*. For well over 70 percent of the book, I could not comprehend the scientific information, yet I could scarcely lay the book aside. The subject matter enthralled me, despite the fact that I could not intellectually grasp the meaning. It left me with a sense of cosmic wonder that insinuated meaning into the depth of my being. It is one of the most compelling books I have ever read.

Similarly with Teilhard. Perhaps it was the vision rather than the message—or the vision mediated through the message—that intrigued me. That sense of elegant movement of God's Spirit in the unceasing unfolding of life. And I began to get the evolutionary significance as I started to research the story of human origins. Now I could see evolution at work with a scope and depth that vastly expanded every fiber of my wisdom and curiosity.

I had heard of Charles Darwin and the neo-Darwinians, but their take on evolution and its impact on universal life seemed cold and mechanistic. It lacked the dynamism and spiritual value of the Teilhardian approach. Many years later, Darwin and his various followers began to make a great deal more sense.

When I first began exploring human evolution, Louis and Mary Leaky were the big names, and their discovery of *Homo Habilis* (the handy person) in 1959 was the primary evidence pointing to a date of origins, some two million years ago. That realization utterly fascinated me. Nor did I experience any conflict with my inherited religious wisdom, dogmatically asserting a sin-infested humanity of a mere few thousand years, whose human and evolutionary meaning all depended on the divine rescue of Jesus a mere two thousand years ago.

I grew up with a Christian view suggesting that it was what evolved after the time of Jesus that was really important, indeed the only evolutionary time-scale of any divine or human significance. As for the Hebrew Scriptures, their main significance related to the story of creation outlined in the opening chapters of the book of Genesis. Up until the mid-twentieth century, most Christians around the world took the creation sequence in Genesis as literal fact, with a date for the entire creation—and not merely humans—at around 5000 BCE.[1]

The study of human origins officially known as *paleoanthropology*—a subbranch of paleontology (denoting the study of animal fossils)—began in the nineteenth century[2] but only attained its full scientific rigor in the latter half of the twentieth century. We now know that our species has been on the earth for an estimated seven million years, blossoming into the more distinctive hominoid status at least 3.3 million years ago. Despite the scientific verification and validation of this knowledge, the religions of the world—as well as Christian theology—have scarcely begun to engage with this enlarged human horizon.[3]

Thanks to the growing acquaintance with cosmology and modern science, the ancient date of 13.7 billion years has become almost a household term. In the United States alone an estimated ten million people have been exposed to the "new cosmology" and are inspired by this expansive view. Yet the United States continues to have deeply divided ideologies between the creationists and the evolutionists. The visionary information in the public arena has yet to percolate to the depths of human consciousness.

Teilhard de Chardin has been a major influence in my life, particularly in my spiritual and theological coming of age. His expanded horizon of spiritual possibility, deeply earthly, on the one hand, while stretching the human spirit toward cosmic consciousness, on the other, captures something of the grand adventure that has been the story of my life. For me, and for many others, Teilhard opened the creative horizons of our evolving universe.

Central Features

I want to focus attention here on three central dynamics of evolution: *growth*, *change*, and *complexity*. These same dynamics characterize my own life story from beginning to end. My inherited formation, from both a human and a faith perspective, heavily emphasized the unchanging nature of life. Keep things the same as much as possible and for as long as possible. And I was frequently reminded: the essentials never change.

In my psychology studies, in the late 1970s, a significant shift was taking place in our understanding of human growth. The earlier emphasis on the childhood foundations was giving way to the perception that growth happens across the entire lifespan. Given the right conditions, people can change behavior significantly across all the various life stages. Around that same time, the developmental psychologist James Fowler was integrating the new developmental understandings into the acquisition and growth of faith in the human life cycle. I return to his insights later in this chapter.

Stability has never featured strongly in my life; the older I become the more I encounter daily challenges to integrate change and new perspectives. Observing the natural world we inhabit, the plant, the tree, and the animal never remain the same. Everything grows, unfolds into ever new ways of being. We can't control such change; indeed, the only authentic response we can make is to learn to flow with it.

In the change we experience around and within us, there is another inescapable dimension: *decay*, *decline*, and *death*. Such disintegration is not an evil, nor is it the consequence of sin stated in Romans 6:23, but it is a God-given dimension of all creation. Without the disintegration and death of the old there can be no true novelty. The ability to let go of that which previously sustained us is a perquisite for embracing the new that morphs into further growth and development.

Sometimes, we are left with the impression that things die out completely. In fact, the second law of thermodynamics claims that such termination is the destiny of all organic life. The piece of coal thrown into the fire can never be restored to its original form. An important transformation takes place, however, as the burning of that coal generates heat energy that propels technology to create a range of new entities. The piece of coal has not come to naught. Its true identity as an energy-bearing structure continues in a range of new forms, which cannot be perceived, understood, or accessed in the original form of the piece of coal.

Viewing the natural world around us, we see things growing, a vast range of life-forms becoming and developing through greater complexity. It is often an untidy, even messy process (hence, the notion of chaos) and certainly does not follow a neat, logical progression. Any process of development involving increasing levels of complexity, elegance, and beauty will be accompanied by a considerable amount of destruction and waste. At every level of life, creation and destruction are interwoven in evolution's trajectory.[4] (I return to this insight in chapter four.)

The Lure of the Future

As if all the above elements of *growth*, *change*, and *complexity* were not enough to come to terms with, there is the additional factor of directionality. The inherited neo-Darwinian claim is that evolution happens by repeating the successful patterns of the past; in other words, everything is driven from behind. Formal religions also adopt this view. Truth rests primarily in that which has stood the test of time.

Although offered primarily as a theological supplement to our inherited scientific understanding, the notion that evolutionary unfolding responds to a future lure, and is not based merely on past influence, helps to explain the rapidity and complexity of evolution today. Just as human beings are motivated, not merely by former successes, but by the attraction of as-yet-unrealized possibilities, so in the wider realm of life we detect breakthroughs that cannot simply be explained by referencing the past.

The scientific notion of the strange attractor comes into play here. According to chaos theory, alongside the turbulence and randomness that characterize many organic systems is the often-unexpected emergence of orderliness. The new sense of order seems to emerge from within the system itself, strangely drawn into the structure that has come to be known as a strange attractor. When a new behavior reaches a critical threshold, unexpectedly it spills over to the benefit of the entire species.

The human hunger for transcendence toward ultimate meaning can also be understood as another feature of the lure of the future. In the words of Ilia Delio, "If God makes things to make themselves (as Thomas Aquinas suggested) then self making is written into the heart of nature. Reality is a process constituted by the drive for transcendence. The nature of reality is to explore possibilities that are not yet actual. Nature, in a sense, is never satisfied; it is always on for novelty and to be something more.... Every human life is the cosmos winding its way into the future."[5]

Theologically, I understand that the central attraction of the lure of the future is a fruit and wisdom of the Holy Spirit. The Spirit can be understood as a kind of cosmic strange attractor. Throughout this book, I explore the meaning of the Holy Spirit in terms of what indigenous peoples all over our world call the *Great Spirit.* This is probably the oldest insight into the meaning of God known to humans. For indigenous peoples the Great Spirit is not a transcendent being above and outside creation but rather the energizing creativity that lures all beings into creative engagement with life. And for our First Nations peoples that happens primarily in and through the land (soil). The land itself is imbued with vital empowering energy, making it a "strange attractor" for the awakening and evolution of our spiritual selves.

Today, evolution is the most generic name we can give to this divine-human partnership energizing the entire web of life. Creation itself is not some fixed physical entity but an emergent process, forever open to new becoming. In and through the earth, and not apart from it, we work out our "salvation," a traditional Christian term that takes on a whole new meaning, as we will illustrate in chapter four.

Evolutionary Integration

The popular appeal of an evolutionary perspective in our time may well be related to several new invitations to integration confronting us as a species; perhaps these are the strange attractors of our time! The dominant role we have adopted ever since the agricultural revolution (some ten thousand years ago) is proving to be highly destructive, not merely for other life-forms but for ourselves as well, as suggested by the coronavirus of 2020, implicating marketing procedures with bats, birds, and animals.

The evolutionary imperative of this time is calling for more informed adaptations and adjustments in how we relate with other life-forms and with the vitality of creation itself. There is a shift that is becoming increasingly clear, namely, that humans cannot evolve in a truly creative way without bringing with us in a more convivial way a range of other creatures we have long regarded as mere fodder to serve our personal needs.

How to reclaim the animal within and without is one such invitation to new integration, one that has been of major concern to theologians throughout the opening years of the twenty-first century.[6] In my own early spiritual development, the need to subdue and get rid of the animal within was deemed to be foundational to all spiritual growth. The animal denoted the instinctual drives, deemed to be alien to God's grace and holiness. The animal was extensively associated with the demonic at work in the human heart.

The kind of dualistic splitting at work here can be traced back to Aristotle and classical Greek anthropology, where the human is declared to be endowed with a soul superior to all other life-forms.

Today, it is the integration of the animal—along with the plant and other organic organisms—that is coming to the fore in our more integrated understanding of both theology and spirituality.

The fascination with our cosmological significance, despite our tiny place within it, quickly moved into our need to wrestle with our dysfunctional relationship with the home planet, our Earth. Gradually, we came to recognize that we are Earthlings, creatures that belong to the earth; we are totally dependent on it, not merely for survival, but for all the resources made available to us for growth and flourishing. It is at this juncture that a disconnect with formal religion first came to the surface. Instead of waiting for the promised liberation of a life hereafter, where our hopes and dreams would be fulfilled, a substantial shift in consciousness took place—and its fuller impact continues to happen. *It is in our identity and status as Earthlings that God works primarily in and through us.* Our earthiness, rather than our promised heavenly escape, is the basis of all that is sacred within and around us.[7]

None of the major religions have yet come to terms with this evolutionary shift. Many are not even aware of it. Along with our politicians, economists, and social policy makers, our ecclesiastical leaders are in deep denial of this new focus. It is indeed scary to confront the fact that many of our long-held cultural assumptions are outliving their usefulness and need to be consigned to the archives of history. The lure of the future (outlined above) is inviting us all to a new evolutionary threshold wherein it will be open-ended possibilities, rather than past securities, that provide more solid foundations for hope and meaning.

Engaging Evolution's Paschal Journey

All of which brings us to the central theme of this book. On the one hand, I am offering reflections on personal experiences of the paschal journey at work in my own life over many years. It has become increasingly clear, however, that many, if not all, of those personal encounters with decline and death leading to new life were entwined with the wider evolutionary shifts outlined above. The personal and transpersonal seem to be inescapably interconnected, particularly within the co-evolutionary imperative of our time.[8] Sr. Ilia Delio synthesizes the challenge in this cryptic statement: "Evolution is the rise of transpersonal life, one cosmic person in formation whom Christians call the Christ."[9] The Christian context alluded to here is wonderfully elaborated in Richard Rohr's *The Universal Christ*.

Each chapter of this book follows a double dynamic. I begin with personal narrative, indicating evolutionary growth in my own life story, usually a narrative of success but often intermingled with challenge and struggle. Then follows the transpersonal dimension in which the evolutionary process of the personal narrative is interwoven with a corresponding process on the larger scale of life, whether in the cosmic or planetary domains.

I am adopting this strategy to highlight the deep interconnection between person and planet (universe). Everything in the human body has been given to us from the body of creation. The energy that begets and sustains life on the grand universal scale is that same creative energy that empowers each person, in fact, every organic creature. As we move deeper into the twenty-first century, all the sciences—and religions—will need to wrestle with this evolving earth-centered anthropology.

Central to this enterprise is my desire to integrate more consciously the paradox of birth-death-rebirth that recurs at every level of life, human and cosmic alike. Throughout the book, I describe it in the traditional Christian language of the *paschal journey*.[10] Although the language is Christian in origin, the phenomenon I am describing is universal and has been at work since the dawn of creation. This paradoxical dynamic of creation-cum-destruction did not begin with Jesus of Nazareth; it long predated him. In undergoing the process of Calvary-cum-resurrection, Jesus was undertaking his own evolution, a process already operative throughout the entire creation.

From the Personal to the Transpersonal

In my interweaving of the personal and the transpersonal, I am seeking out a more organic way to reconstruct human meaning. Many of our problems at this time arise from a dysfunctional anthropology. The human project has lost its authentic sense of direction, painfully illustrated in the COVID-19 pandemic of 2020. We have become an imperial violent species, setting ourselves above and beyond everything else in creation. Instead of being grounded in the cosmic-planetary web of life, we have set ourselves over against it, treating every other life form as a mere commodity existing for our use and benefit. Such a dysfunctional relationship is unsustainable and currently plunging humanity into one crisis after another.

In our deluded anthropocentricism, we invented religion to resolve the perversity that we ourselves created. That delusional travesty is cryptically captivated by the Episcopalian bishop John Shelby Spong in his book *Biblical Literalism*: "Atonement theology assumes that we were created in some kind of original perfection. We now know that life has emerged from a single cell that evolved into self-conscious complexity over billions of years. *There was no original perfection,* so there could never have been a fall from perfection (emphasis mine)." This important shift of perspective belongs to an evolutionary understanding of life and faith.

Already I am launching the reader into the grand evolutionary narrative of the human species. In the latter half of the twentieth century, we experienced a seismic shift in our evolutionary understanding of life. Quantum physics, the new cosmology, Gaia theory, and the new biology all opened up novel vast arenas

of understanding. Our narrow mechanistic paradigms, and sin-laden religious ideologies, often dated within a mere few thousand years, were expanded into time-scales of millions and even billions of years. The evolutionary imperative is central to the vastly expanded horizons engaging the contemporary imagination.

We Are Being Evolved

Tragically the very word *evolution* still evokes a negative and, at times, a highly convoluted response among evangelical Christians (and others) around our world. The fear seems to be that we are undermining the creative primacy of God. The real reason, however, is the threat to that brand of human imperialism that likes to play God. In so many cases, we have invented a God image, modeled on our patriarchal projections, seeking absolute control for ourselves. We need to let that ideology die out. In fact, it is already dying, and that fuels even more the irrational fear of those who invest so much in it. Sadly all the major religions, and particularly the three monotheistic faiths (Judaism, Christianity, Islam), cling to it tenaciously. The God-given reality of evolutionary creativity is too much for them to embrace.

Meanwhile, millions of people all over our world are riding the wave of this new emergence. Some remain consciously religious, in a variety of different ways, but many have either abandoned or outgrown the faith that one time felt important. I have had the privilege of walking alongside many of these new explorers. Although viewed by many churches and religions as drifters or postmodern lost souls, I believe they are evolutionary catalysts, touching depths of the paschal journey that elude several of our ardent religionists. They are the companions I cherish as I unravel my own engagement with the paschal journey in our world today.

Much of this personal narrative feels like the birthing of new vision and novel paradigms for our contemporary understanding of life and its meaning. And yet, such birthing is intimately connected with death and dying. How the two strands, the creative dynamic evolution of birth and death, are inseparably interwoven—as, indeed, they have been for much of my life story—is the central theme of this autobiographical narrative. In fact, I suspect they feature with equal complexity in every person's life. My hope is that what I share here will help others to walk that same pathway, to embrace what might well be the greatest paradox of all life-forms: dying as a precondition for rising into new life.

CHAPTER TWO

In the Shadow of Religious Fear

> *Our task must be to free ourselves from this prison by widening our circle of compassion, to embrace all living creatures and the whole of nature in its beauty.*
>
> —Albert Einstein

In the fall of 1995, I participated in a workshop for a group of missionaries, my one and only visit to Taiwan. The one-day event commenced with an individual exercise requiring each of us to fill in a questionnaire, titled a Bioregional Quiz.[11] It consisted of twenty questions around issues like the sources of one's daily food; the grasses, plants, animals inhabiting a particular locality; recycling of waste products; local methods of agriculture, and so on. In terms of my childhood home in rural Ireland I could answer seventeen of the twenty questions. At the time, however, I was living in London and had been in the same place for over five years; in terms of my London location, I could only answer six of the twenty questions.

The point of the exercise was to establish how well we knew our local *bioregions*. At the time I was not even sure what the concept of bioregionalism meant. The exercise clearly indicated that in terms of my London home I was poorly grounded in my bioregion, whereas in my childhood home of rural Ireland I was intimately interconnected with the surrounding environment.

Through a Glass Darkly

I want to situate my childhood within the context of the *paschal journey*, even before I offer a theoretical and theological explanation of the notion of the paschal journey. I was born into a very poor family, like most rural families in Ireland of the 1950s. My parents struggled to survive and maintain a minimum standard of health and well-being for themselves and for their five children, of which I was the eldest.

Despite the obvious struggle, when it came to basic necessities we were largely self- sufficient. We had four cows that gave us the milk and cream we needed, along with thirty hens, producing eggs and families of young chicks, which my mother sold at the local market. We grew a few acres of wheat (corn), which was crushed into flour at the local mill; from that my mother baked all the bread we consumed. Once a year we grew a potato crop, our staple diet for a whole year, and once a year, we killed a pig, providing the meat for the entire family. Some of our neighbors had sheep, from whose wool the spinner-woman in the local village knitted our sweaters and socks. And from the local piece of bogland we obtained the turf to keep the home fire aflame. That fire was not merely a source of heat and comfort in cold weather; it was also base for all heating and cooking. For the greater part we were self-sufficient.

Against that background, I knew my bioregion intimately, many years before the ecological awakening that would become a major part of my life and my faith.

Today, some people might describe it as an idyllic childhood, deeply immersed in the intimacy and sacredness of nature. Every field had a name. Each animal was distinctly unique. We loved the rhythms of the seasons and enjoyed life amid a range of simple pleasures. We never celebrated birthdays, and rarely did we receive or exchange any gifts. In my mother's words: money was too tight, meaning that it had to be kept for the essentials.

We went to church every Sunday, and at home said the rosary every night, always ending with the Act of Contrition, in case we might die during the night. We had a strong sense of God's loving care and protection, but much stronger (at least for me) was that watchful judge above the sky, noting every sin we committed and by whom we would be judged at the end of time.

At age twelve, I went to boarding school, run by the Missionaries of the Sacred Heart, the religious congregation (order) I subsequently joined. This gave me the privilege of a second-level education; only my younger sister and myself had that privilege. While many of my classmates hated boarding school, to me it felt exciting and special. For the first time in my life, I tasted sausages and relished tinned beans; I watched movies and read books. And I did well in my exams!

I well remember the year 1960, shortly before my thirteenth birthday. Various millenarian movements had been foretelling the end of the world for that ominous year. I cannot recall where I learned of all that speculation, but I do recall the dread and fear it engendered in me, particularly in October 1962 when news of the Cuban Missile Crisis emerged. We were told that this might well be the end of the world, and what a relief when the end did not transpire. Piled together in that petrified religiosity were a number of beliefs that my innocent and naïve mind took literally:

God was a harsh and severe judge.

Death was a great curse incurred by human sinfulness.

The first judgment happened at death, but the second one at the end of the world would be much more severe.

Jesus came to die for sinners, but apparently that did little to mitigate God's judgment.

The resurrection had something to do with the divinity of Jesus, rather than human salvation.

The paschal journey, if it had any meaning in this schema, referred to the prayer and penance that were essential for good faith, particularly during the Lenten season.

My childhood interest in priesthood grew stronger, and I felt at home in the missionary congregation I had gotten to know during my time at their boarding school. Upon completing my second-level education, I went straight to novitiate, a special spiritual year to launch candidates into the road for priesthood and, in this case, religious life as well. The novitiate was meant to be a year of intense spiritual experience and quite ascetical lifestyle, cut off as far as possible from the outside (sinful) world. For me, it felt like a test of endurance, and I suffered a great deal from religious scruples. I was happy to see it end.

Next followed my first year studying scholastic philosophy, in a remote seminary in rural Ireland. Despite the fact that I was struggling spiritually and intellectually, I managed to see the year through, occasionally bemused by those among my classmates who loved bantering about philosophical quagmires like the meaning of a dead dog—if it is dead what is its "doggyness"? Who the hell cares!

The City of Light

I was in my twentieth year. Life up to now felt like being in a darkened container, peering out at an unknown world, somewhat mesmerized by it all ("through the glass darkly"). As I journeyed through therapy in later years, I encountered several painful elements of those impoverished childhood and adolescent years. Only in more recent times have I come to recognize those formative years as a dark night of soul and senses, and in true mystical fashion, I can now see I was being prepared (purified) for a breakthrough with several key features of a paschal journey.

For my second year of scholastic philosophy, my religious congregation decided to open a formation house (seminary) in the capital city of Dublin, so that we could avail of an intercongregational formation program initiated by the Jesuits in Milltown Park, Dublin. I can still recall the evening of my arrival as we drove the streets of Dublin, enamored by the bright orange-yellow street lighting! Light was beginning to penetrate my darkness. Seeds of resurrection were beginning to sprout from the long arid Calvary of my childhood and adolescence.

Within a matter of days, I felt completely at home in this new environment, and I began to find my way around the city as if I had long known it.

Ahead of me was one of the richest years of my life in terms of contentment, growth, and integration. Philosophy continued to be quite a struggle—too abstract and cerebral—but the energy of my new location found a remedy to that dilemma. The Milltown Park Institute provided me with an array of books that opened up new vistas of resurrection breakthrough. The writings of the then-Jesuit theologian Ladislaus Boros changed my understanding of both humanity and God.[12]

Boros was describing a Christian anthropology, prioritizing the sacredness and wholeness of the human condition above and beyond the flawed nature I had internalized in my earlier years. This not only was refreshing and reassuring but also launched me into an incarnational sense of meaning that engages my mind and spirit to the present day. It was indeed a stone rolled away from the tomb.

And it began to change my imaging of God. The God of our deep humanity—wounded indeed, but more magnificently healed—could not have been that distant harsh judge I had taken so literally in my earlier years. It felt like my image of God had also been released from the tomb. It would be several years later before I would name the spiritual encounter awakening in my soul. It was—and fortunately continues to be—the God of unconditional love, manifested uniquely in the human face of Jesus.

The second author whose writings transposed me onto mystical heights was the already-referenced Jesuit paleontologist, Teilhard de Chardin.[13] His vision proved to be the icing on the cake for the grounding of my faith, perhaps a subliminal reclaiming of the bioregional connectedness I had known as a child. It was, however, the evolutionary threshold of Teilhard's vision that captivated my imagination, leading me into the deep recesses of our ancient human becoming amid the wilds of Africa. Unknown to myself I was on the way to becoming a planetary citizen and a cosmic mystic.

By now I had come to realize that I was carrying baggage from my past that needed to be discarded. The realization that this would need to be done in a therapeutic context dawned on me only when I began my social science studies in my late twenties. What began to happen—either by grace or by chance (probably a bit of both)—was a kind of working backward. I realized that all I had learned in my novitiate was of little use to me, spiritually or humanly. So, all that had to be unlearned. And with it came a sense of healing, deeper meaning, and greater coherence.

Embracing Theology

By the end of that second year of philosophy I was indeed ready for theology, not in terms of what I had learned from philosophy (which in truth was very little) but from the enormous transformative experience of that magnificent year in the city of Dublin and in the Milltown Institute. Theology itself was to become the primary source of my evolving spiritual maturation.

Theology began with my first experience of synchronicity,[14] and fortunately many more were to follow. The very first course I did in theology was on "Death and the Last Things." The professor, a cherished member of my own religious congregation, adopted as a basic text *The Mystery of Death*, authored by none other than the inspiring Ladislaus Boros. It was some years later before I consciously acknowledged the guiding light that was at work in my life. Nor did I realize the paschal journey dynamic that was endemic to it all. Unknown to me or to any of my fellow students, my theology professor was a chronic alcoholic who would die of cirrhosis of the liver six years later at the young age of forty-four.

Theology continued to be a thrilling experience, as the mystery of life and the reality of God were ever more deeply insinuated into my soul. Life also had its moments of struggle and difficulty, but now I felt there was a solid foundation with the aid of which I could weather many a storm. More accurately, I had come to a place in my life journey where I knew I was being held within the power of a mystery that is ultimately benign. That awareness was crucially important as I encountered my first serious crisis of vocation. It happened during my second year of theology and we will pick up that autobiographical nugget in chapter four.

I made my final profession of vows and was duly ordained a priest. Now with the security of ordination behind me, I began to plunge deeper into my understanding of religious life. A visit to the international, ecumenical community in Taizé (France) proved to be another graced breakthrough. In fact, I seriously considered joining the monastery there but finally chose not to. My three weeks at Taizé, involving conversations with monks and others, raised questions around the meaning of my vocation that would engage me for the rest of my life. I came home from Taizé with a clear unambiguous conviction that I was first and foremost a religious and only secondarily a priest. My vocation to religious life took on enormous significance.

Mystical Intuition

It was on that same visit to Taizé that I first began to realize an awakening sense of mysticism in my life. On the early morning after my arrival, as I was exploring the outline of the monastery and its grounds, I drifted into the underground chapel and sat in the dimly lit, quiet space. I could hear echoes of human breathing, and after my eyes had adjusted to the relative darkness, I could see some people stretched out of the floor asleep. I felt uneasy that they had chosen this sacred space for sleeping, but a persistent inner voice assured me that it was OK for them to be there. The words of the transfiguration story, "Lord, it is good for us to be here" (Matthew 17:4), kept resonating in my psyche.

Having sat and enjoyed the tranquility for some thirty minutes, and now with my eyesight adjusted to the relative darkness, I was drawn to a number of icons that hung on the surrounding walls. To my left was one that looked like an image of Mary, as Our Lady of Perpetual Succor, to which I had a strong childhood devotion. As I drew closer I recognized the image, not that of Mary, but, to my amazement, an image of the transfiguration, with the words written underneath: "Lord, it is good for us to be here."

Throughout my entire time at Taizé I kept encountering those same words, either literally, vocally, or subliminally. On August 5 I arrived back in the United Kingdom. One of my priest-colleagues asked me if I would celebrate Eucharist the following morning in a nearby convent, and in preparation for that I went to the sacristy to check out the liturgy for the day—the Feast of the Transfiguration (August 6). Synchronicity at work again!

Only some years later when I went back to Taizé did I realize the fuller impact of what was transpiring at that time. As I shared my story with some of the Taizé Brothers, I was informed that the icon of the transfiguration was never on the wall of the underground chapel. They were also quick to reassure me that it was not my imagination running wild. Something much deeper was unfolding, a grace for which I am eternally grateful.

It was on that first visit to Taizé that I decided to write a book on my evolving understanding of religious life. For me Taizé marked a rediscovery of my vocation and an affirmation of my emerging adult faith. That first visit truly felt like a resurrection experience—and in keeping with what was now becoming a more identifiable rhythm in my life, it was also a preparation for other Calvarys. The paschal journey never ceases!

From the Personal to the Transpersonal

Throughout this autobiographical narrative, I want to keep a responsible balance between the personal and the transpersonal. Without the transpersonal, the personal can too easily become incestuous and self-inflationary, a deluded ego trip. Grace is always inviting us outward and beyond the limited confines of our own ego world.

Taizé opened me up to an enlarged world, expanding the horizons of my faith, paving the way for an integration that is beyond our mere human competence. Today, those enlarged horizons are the stuff that millions engage with, thanks to the culture of mass information within which we all live. Scholars do the expanding in terms of their expertise—theologically and scripturally—but the Spirit blows across a vast landscape where the boundary between the expert and the ordinary believer grows ever closer.

A childlike codependency was central to the understanding of faith that brought me through childhood, adolescence, and indeed right into my years as a young adult. Then a significant shift took place, not of my making, but through a set of circumstances deeply interwoven with graced wisdom. Evolution had landed me into a new developmental sphere. The transpersonal was at work, and I was reborn into a more adult sense of my emerging faith.

Evolving an Adult Faith

Growing into a more adult way of understanding and living my faith did not—in my case—result in many major religious adjustments. It all happened in what seems to have been a gradual, organic process. The evolutionary vision of Teilhard de Chardin was certainly a major influence. It reinforced the integration of the human and the holy that I first encountered in the writings of Ladislaus Boros. More important, Teilhard's vision enabled me to build bridges across the dualistic split between the sacred and the secular. In a few years that led me into the exploration of quantum physics and the expanded vision of the new cosmology.

Meanwhile, Teilhard's evolutionary insights led me along a more anthropological route, the unfolding story of the human species across several million years. With hindsight, I can now see that this is where my adult believer came into its own. The Christian notion of incarnation took on a whole new meaning, and while few theologians seemed interested (then or now), something deep within assured me that this was a faith journey worth pursuing. I was beginning to trust adult wisdom coming from within.

Trusting my inner wisdom was never a purely individual pursuit. I began riding the wave of a great story, which fortunately I trusted to a point where it led me ever more deeply into a transformed spiritual consciousness. At this juncture, the distinction between religion and spirituality became all important. It was all too clear that my ancient ancestors, going back some one hundred thousand years were already operating out of an informed spiritual sense of life. Long before formal religions evolved (about five thousand years ago), members of the human species were exploring spiritual meaning in several contexts of their daily lives. And they were doing so without rabbis, bishops, or imams, and without any of the patriarchal structures adopted by major religions.

When I began exploring our long human story in the 1970s, the science of human origins (paleontology) had not yet evolved into the rigorous science it is today, as outlined briefly in chapter one. It is when the scholars moved into Ethiopia in the 1980s, and research became more expansive in Kenya, Tanzania, and later Chad, that the momentum gathered to the point of establishing the current date for our human origins, namely, that of seven million years ago.

This is now our sacred story, the expanded horizon of our faith as adult people of God. Africa, and not the land of Israel, is where God first incarnated in our embodied spirits. This is our graced narrative as God's creatures, and our God has been with us on this long journey every step of the way.

This is the adult coming of age, outgrowing the former codependent relationship of the docile child obeying the patriarchal God-father. We are called to co-create with our God and not merely for "Him."

In that co-creative process, our engagement is deeply rooted in the soil of planet Earth. As Earthlings, our true God-given home is the living creation itself, in its cosmic and planetary dimensions. In this adult understanding there is no room for the vale of tears from which religion has long told us to escape.

We are birthed into life in the empowering grace of our creative God, and our collaborative responsibility with that God is to birth anew the nature that has birthed us. In this co-creative process, there is no room for patriarchal power or manipulation. It is our sense of belonging that defines our true nature and our God-given identity. That to which we belong defines the very essence of our adult selves.

Therefore, God's will for humans—and for all creation—is to exercise an agency of co-creation: to bring about on earth a greater fullness, the evolutionary complexity I described in chapter one. We are meant to be an engaged and involved species, adult people serving an adult God, in the ever-evolving enterprise of our magnificent universe. Seeking to escape to a life hereafter makes no evolutionary sense anymore; in fact, it never did for our ancient ancestors.

Adult Challenges for Contemporary Faith

Religious faith today is in deep crisis and rapidly losing credibility all over our world. We are witnessing a classical evolutionary shift, featuring a paschal journey of dying, with seeds of new life beginning to appear. Contrary to the scholarly tendency of the new atheism (for example, Christopher Hitchens and Richard Dawkins) to dismiss religious observance in the modern world, we must note that an estimated 50 percent of the human species (some 3.5 billion people) practice one or another religion in deep loyalty to their respective traditions. To the fore are Muslims, fundamentalist Christians, an estimated 70 percent of Hindus, and a diverse array of Buddhists (mainly through meditation practices). The Muslim religion seems to be on the increase and becoming ever more attractive to younger people seeking clarity, simplicity, and an outlet for heroic living.

Today, rapidly increasing numbers of people drift away from religious belief and from allegiance to one or another denomination. We need to distinguish those who drift from those who reject. The latter often resemble people who choose to end a destructive relationship, because it is no longer considered to be life-giving. Such rejection may be temporary, but frequently they do not return. Some will move to another denomination, for example, from Catholic to Protestant (or vice versa); others change their religion, for example, from Christian to Muslim. And, finally, we witness the growing amorphous body of those who claim to be spiritual but not religious, an evolutionary movement of the twenty-first century deserving a far deeper assessment than is usually granted.

Regarding those who drift away, a key issue here is that of *relevance*. Religion seems neither relevant nor useful anymore. People feel they can get on fine without it. A significant influence here is that of our information-saturated world, in which the desire to know is growing exponentially. In such a culture we witness an ever-deepening curiosity, a tendency to question just about everything, and an adult expectation of honest, truthful answers to questions asked. Additionally, our growing scientific and technological culture tends to provide rational explanations replacing mythological or religious beliefs of former times.

Most of the adults who have graced my life, those that have embraced the search for a more adult way of living out the faith, are better described as trans-religious rather than postreligious. Some may abandon entirely the religion they have inherited, and some may maintain a minimal rate of practice, going to church at Christmas and Easter and availing of church services for funerals and weddings. The majority, however, maintain strong links, while all the time desiring, and striving for, an experience of church that will honor and nourish their hunger for adult faith.

This yearning emerges out of a twofold adult maturation. First, there is the growing sense of unease and suspicion around the inadequacies of long-held convictions and beliefs and a dissatisfaction with what is preached and delivered at regular church services. Second, is the intellectual awakening and curiosity of our culture of mass information in which people question several aspects of inherited truth (for example, the literal truth of scripture) and seek out forums where they can air their doubts, have their questions heard, and receive responses that invite deeper exploration.

For many such people, the distinction between religion and spirituality is all important. The institutional nature of religion and the perceived rigidity of its doctrines fail to deliver the deeper truth emerging from their life experience. Their hunger for God, and for spiritual meaning, opens up a wider and deeper arena, often described today as *spirituality*.

Although it has been around since the 1960s, the post-religious culture often described as *spirituality* is still poorly understood and often superficially dismissed by those committed to formal religion. Frequently denounced as a by-product of our selfie culture, the movement is perceived as a classical postmodern mixture of "anything goes."

Spirituality can simply be defined as *Spirit connecting with spirit.*[15] From the human perspective it views humans as foundationally open to transcendence, to an intuitive sense of the sacred within oneself and in the surrounding creation. In ancient times it was identified as animism, viewed by religionists as paganism and therefore contrary to God's desire for humanity as understood by the religions. The depth and richness of this ancient sense of the sacred can be authentically understood only when we come to terms with our long evolutionary story as a human species, dating back some seven million years. Assuming that God has been fully at work in us during all that time, and bearing in mind that formal religions (as we know them today) are little more than five thousand years old, then we discern more clearly what we mean by spirituality and its substantial significance in the human story long before formal religions ever evolved.

God: Dying and Rising

Indoctrinated, as many of us are, with the negative appraisal of primal faith, we widely associate our ancient ancestors with the worship of false gods, with idolatry and paganism. Adult people of faith feel and perceive along different lines. They go for depth and seek to honor the wisdom of deep time, whether understood in cosmic, planetary, or anthropological terms. For them God is an open question[16] and not a reality that can be determined by the prevailing philosophical and cultural assumptions of the past few thousand years.

All the formal religions we know today, including Christianity, evolved under the shadow of the postagricultural era, with its heavy emphasis of human domination, control, manipulation, and commodification of the land. This was the era of the Sky God, a human projection empowering the mighty imperial ruler to sanction and validate all that the earthly imperial forces themselves declared to be normative. It is a tragic cultural reductionism that has wreaked havoc on deeper and more ancient spiritual meaning.

Contemporary spirituality—unknowingly for the greater part—is seeking to retrieve a more ancient grounding in the mystery of God, described by several contemporary indigenous peoples as the *Great Spirit*. In all probability, this is the oldest—and deepest—intuition into the meaning of God that we humans possess. In this intuitive understanding, the Spirit is the primary energizer of everything in creation (as intimated in the opening chapter of the book of Genesis) and impacts on human experience through the living vitality of the earth itself.

This reappropriation of the Holy One, re-visioned as the Great Spirit, raises a range of urgent theological questions, which are beginning to engage the scholarly imagination but are already being entertained by adult believers across the contemporary world. The implications are best accessed by reviewing the major theological paradigm shifts happening in our time.

Today, we evidence three theological paradigms at work in our world. The reader will recognize the first two; I hope by the end of this book, the relevance and meaning of the third paradigm will become much clearer.

First, I outline what I name as *the codependent paradigm*, described simply as Creation—Fall—Redemption. The central emphasis here is on the flawed nature of everything in creation. Although it is God's creation, God cannot rectify the fall, attributed to human recklessness (an irrational craving for power), so Jesus is missioned to rescue the flawed reality, a task that continues in the life of the Church, often ensuing in humans entangled in several codependent relationships—hence, a primary reason why humans maturing into a more adult consciousness tend to walk away from such an unhealthy faith system.

The second landscape I name as *the imperial Judeo-Christian paradigm*, which runs like this: Creation—Israel—Jesus—Church—Eschaton. More central to this paradigm is the rescuing imperial

God of the Hebrew Scriptures, modeled primarily on the great King David, who in turn becomes the messianic model for Jesus. That same kingly royal imperative permeates Christianity up to our own time. Although vehemently denounced and opposed by Jesus, the Roman emperor Constantine reestablished the imperial prerogative that then morphed into popes, bishops, and exclusive male clergy, with accompanying institutions to uphold patriarchal power. Of course, it will never truly satisfy authentic spiritual desire, in which case we need the eschatological clause assuring us that God will eventually bring the whole thing to an end in a final act of divine deliverance.

The third landscape is often described as postconfessional and has a radically different feel to it; even the language will initially seem strange. I name it as *the evolutionary paradigm*. It goes like this: Spirit—Energy—Creation—Evolution—Incarnation—Spirituality. Looks like we have dropped the very word *God*! No explicit reference to Father, Jesus, or Holy Spirit, but fret not, they are included. No allusion to fall, redemption, church, or eschaton. And the reader may already be wondering what has happened to revelation and the inspiration of sacred scripture. On top of all that, it looks rather impersonal![17]

The myth of origin is crucial here, as indeed it is for every faith system. Beyond the *ex nihilo* prerogative of the patriarchal male Creator lies a more ancient creative energy, insinuating the dark deep, out of which the Great Spirit energizes all life—*ex profundis*. As noted above, the Great Spirit is how indigenous peoples around our world name the divine reality (God). Energized by the Great Spirit, the birthing Holy One begets the vast panorama we call creation, setting in motion the irreversible complex trajectory that today we call *evolution*. The evolving creative enterprise eventually gives birth to (incarnates) consciously embodied creatures called humans, for whom the historical Jesus serves as an archetypal model. Finally, I am suggesting that our primary theological responsibility at this time is to name and celebrate that magnificent mythopoetic drama within an empowering spirituality for our age.

Committed Christians are likely to panic when faced with this outline. Jesus falls into third place and loses much of the traditional emphasis on salvation and redemption. In fact, Jesus is being reinscribed within the Gospel vision of the kingdom of God.

Signs of Our Time

To conclude this overview of adult faith in the twenty-first century, I will outline briefly those evolutionary developments that have contributed to this cultural awakening, factors that will impact even more significantly over the next few decades.

1. *The Information Explosion.* As already noted, we are living through a time in which new information and insight bombards us unceasingly. Faced with this challenge, some people panic and seek new contexts to give stability, structure, and reassurance in the face of the postmodern onslaught; these are predominantly the people who seek refuge in fundamentalist religion and tend to support right-wing politics. Others bring down the shutters and try to keep the bombardment at bay, giving prior attention to the demands of their daily domestic duties; for a growing proportion of these people, the ability to make money and become wealthier is a central transcendent value. For those who begin to flow with the information explosion, curiosity is scaled to new heights, and they begin to question everything. Fobbing them off with conventional answers, no matter how dogmatic or scientific, is a waste of time. Unknowingly, they are after

breadth and depth, and the evolutionary impetus in their lives will take them in that direction.

2. *The Demise of Imperialism.* Today there prevails an extensive cynicism toward all imperial systems. Power from the top down is no longer trusted to deliver any sense of meaningful empowerment. Nor do people believe in confronting the corruption of power; instead they tend to veer in the direction of exploring alternative possibilities (next point). Sometimes the option for alternatives will fluctuate within the power structure itself, as in the option for Donald Trump, as a businessman, for American president, or the deluded hope that a military general—in the person of Jair Bolsonaro—might clear up the corruption in Brazil's political system.

3. *The Fragmentation of Patriarchy.* With the demise of imperialism arises growing distrust in all wisdom coming from on high. The alternative desire is for consensual process, employing dialogue, consultative dynamics, and mutual agreement. Truth is perceived to unfold from the collective wisdom, rather than what is delivered from any supreme authority. In religious terms, the retired biblical scholar Walter Brueggemann expresses it thus: "But the Church, with its excessive penchant for dogmatic certitude, and the academy, with its fascination with objective rationality, characteristically stop short of the evidence of communal obedience."[18]

4. *Transcending Codependency.* As people learn the art of communal deep listening, and begin to discover the deeper truth that ensues, they also begin to trust more deeply their inner intuitive wisdom. Some begin to realize the terrible price of earlier life conditioning in which they were effectively treated like passive children and enculturated into a codependency that they now realize is no longer congruent

with their adult status. It is in an attempt to reclaim this sense of adulthood that many people choose to outgrow or abandon their inherited religion.

5. *Reawakening the Suppressed Imagination.* The patriarchal consciousness described above first evolved as a response to the extreme climatic conditions associated with the agricultural revolution some ten thousand years ago. In due course, it evolved into the imperial structures of kings and warriors about six thousand years ago. Finally, it gave birth to the rational mind about three thousand years ago, with Greek philosophy as a dominant catalyst for how this way of thinking was internalized in the Western consciousness. One of the catastrophic effects was the suppression of imagination, intuition, and the power of the symbolic. Today, these qualities are back with a vengeance, creating seismic shifts in the arts, in human sexuality, and in psychic exploration.

6. *The Relational Revolution of Quantum Physics.* Classical science with its focus on rationality, objectivity, and quantification has certainly brought enormous benefits to our world, particularly in the industrial and technological spheres. It has, however, left millions of people with a raw psychic hunger and a cultural isolation from pitting the human over against the natural world. Quantum physics illuminates a very different sense of reality, with creative energy underpinning every life process and the capacity for interconnection foundational to all growth and progress.

Our evolving scientific paradigms inform a new way of being spiritual that is essentially multidisciplinary, nondualistic, and grounded in a much more expansive sense of the sacred. And they incarnate for us a different way of grounding our understanding of God. As we move from the personal to the transpersonal we outgrow what fitted well at earlier life stages. But growth requires change, and change embraces diversity.

And for those among us seeking to honor the evolutionary thrust—as for many adults today—there is no going back. The lure is for the future and not for the past. In Christian terms we call it resurrection, that expansive horizon beckoning at us from every Calvary, as we learn to negotiate the mystical paradox on which all life flourishes.

CHAPTER THREE

Engaging the Paschal Journey of Religious Life

> *Learn and obey the rules very well, so you will know how to break them properly.*
>
> —The Dalai Lama

> *The more conscious the individual becomes, the more individual becomes person, and each person is person only to the extent that the individual freely lives by the life of the whole.*
>
> —Beatrice Bruteau

Today, as I live through the life stage of three-score-and-ten, I recognize a sense of physical decline in my life, with a range of challenges for health and well-being. The dimension of the paschal journey that impacts more strongly and directly, however, is that of the vowed life of which I have been a member for over fifty years. As I ponder the personal challenges of this process and try to discern why so many people either shun or ignore it (particularly male clerics like myself), I realize that it is in this realm more than any other that I have encountered and negotiated a very real sense of dying and rising again on a range of different levels. Indeed, I feel I have spent a great deal of my life engaging this paradoxical journey.

As a seminarian in the early 1970s I sat in a classroom with forty other clerical students. One professor, a Jesuit priest, was introducing us to the challenges of moral theology and how to surface meaning amid a range of ethical dilemmas. One of my classmates veered off the subject and asked about the meaning of religious life (all of us were members of religious orders or congregations). The question was dismissed with an abrupt swipe: "Forget about religious life; that will be dead ten years from now." Wow! Where did that cannonball come from?

Whether because of shock or disbelief—or perhaps downright confusion—nobody in the class picked up the professor's remark; at least no one mentioned it, either within or outside the classroom. For my part, I consigned it to some remote part of my psyche, assuming it would evaporate into thin air. Quite likely that would have happened were it not for the fact that upon returning to the seminary, after our summer recess, over half my class had not come back (they had left religious life), and three of the professors had also departed from both priesthood and religious life, including the professor who had signaled the imminent demise of the vowed life.

At the time, the outrageous suggestion that religious life might have only another ten years landed like an atom bomb. Long before I understood the deeper meaning of the paschal journey, I was now catapulted right into its throes. What is the point of staying if total disintegration is just a short few years away? I did not talk to my formators about the issue but confided in an old saintly Jesuit, who listened with great attention and assured me not to worry too much as all would be well in the hands of Mother Church. But if Mother Church was not good enough for the professor of moral theology, how could she be good enough for me? Despite the loving reassurance

I was given, I was unable to accept it. I guess the "hermeneutic of suspicion" was already fermenting in my soul.

The Rise and Fall of Religious Orders

Instead, I opted for a lonely, individual search, reading everything I could find on religious life, its meaning, and its history. Within a few months I was blessed with a significant breakthrough—seedlings of resurrection on my hill of Calvary! In a little-known religious journal, an Irish sister offered an overview of the history of religious life, based on the historical analysis of a French Jesuit, Raymond Hostie. According to this research, religious life evolved in cycles of approximately three hundred years each, from meager beginnings, maturing into significant presence and achievements, and then moving down the other half of the curve, to eventual extinction (not for all, but for most). And with the present cycle commencing around 1800 CE, now in the closing decades of the twentieth century, things were already moving down in a progressive process of decline and diminution.

Few reviews of Hostie's analysis were positive or affirming. His samples were exclusively male and quite small, and it was all based on evidence from the West (largely from Europe).[19] Despite such dismissals, this way of understanding religious life, and particularly the crisis I was wrestling with, made sense to me. It felt like a light in my soul clearing away the fog of my doubts and illuminating future possibilities full of hope and promise. Intuitively, I knew that I was not dealing with mere rational information, nor was I discouraged by those who dismissed Hostie and his perceived historical limitations. Something deep within told me that here was a truth that would become enormously significant for the rest of my life.

I kept on reading and doing further research. I began to understand more clearly the dynamics at work in each historical cycle, all the time obtaining a clearer perspective on what was happening in the current phase (known as the missionary cycle). It had peaked around 1960, and statistics from Rome confirmed that, as did those indicating the decline since the mid-twentieth century. The moral theology professor was well off the mark. He was right in declaring the potential death of the current model of religious life, but not for at least another one hundred years, rather than his predicted ten years.

The deeper meaning of the paschal journey became so much more transparent. Facing even the worst possible scenario—that my own religious congregation might die out—did not undermine my faith or hope. As each former cycle disappeared, there rose up a range of new groups (resurrection) carrying religious life to new heights of fervor and mission. My congregation may die out, but religious life is sure to survive!

I was saddened by the fact that so few religious were aware of all this, and nobody, it seems, wanted to know. Business as usual seems to have been the veneer, covering a great deal of denial. And in my case, there also prevailed a robust allegiance to patriarchal priesthood, the decline or dying out of which was simply inconceivable. I return to that topic in chapter nine.

Hoping to convert at least some colleagues to my way of seeing things, and desiring to share the hope that felt so important to me—even in the face of the irreversible decline of the vowed life—I began to explore the possibility of publishing a book on the subject. It took a few years and eventually emerged in 1981, with the apt title: *The Seed Must Die...Religious Life, Survival or Extinction.*

It got only a few reviews and those were not very positive. Nonetheless, the book reached across the English-reading world, proving to be a source of wisdom, guidance, and hope for female religious particularly.

As recent as 2015, I had a heartwarming letter from a ninety-five-year-old Dominican Sister, thanking me for writing that book, and to cite her own words: "In times of great doubt, it was the one book that kept me going."

The Vowed Life in Global Crisis

In 1991, Ave Maria Press, in Notre Dame, Indiana, published a much more elaborate version of my original thesis, titled *Religious Life: A Prophetic Vision*. On the strength of that book, I got my first invitations to work in the United States, predominantly with female congregations and a vast spectrum of lay associates. By the mid-1990s, invitations were coming from Australia, Africa, and Asia.

The truth of the paschal journey of religious life was beginning to ring true. Numbers in the West were rapidly declining, and the diminishing impact was often rationalized by noting the still large numbers entering in South/Central America, Africa, and Catholic Asia. As we moved into the twenty-first century, even numbers in the southern hemisphere revealed the beginnings of a downward curve. In the case of Africa, entrants are still quite abundant, but rarely are we told of the hemorrhaging taking place in the increasing numbers that subsequently leave.

My discerning hunch is that the decline that previously affected the West, will, in the course of the twenty-first century, impact the entire Catholic world. This time around, the paschal journey of the vowed life is likely to have global implications. The personal and practical consequences are being explored right across all parts of today's Catholic world. Dealing with decline and diminishment has been surfacing in chapter meetings and assemblies ever since the 1980s. Some groups have already died out; others have created various amalgamations. Some have embraced a more international orientation in the hope that the younger members of the South can come to the rescue of the West. Some still seek out "vocations," but many don't. Some groups have talked about new forms of membership but few have explored this option in practical ways.

There is a tentative acknowledgment of serious decline; yet, nobody talks about dying out. How we might embrace this option proactively and engage with it creatively remains a substantial piece of work still awaiting our attention.

For religious life in the Catholic church we evidence the setting sun, the fading light, the journey into the vast darkness beyond which we know not what exists. There will indeed be a new sunrise, a fresh dawn, and the challenge of other possibilities, many of which are likely to be entirely new. Another cycle will unfold, and in due course another paschal journey will plough a sacred furrow.

From the Personal to the Transpersonal

My education in history—secular and ecclesiastical—was a memory test regarding outstanding wars and heroic victors. It was my encounter with the underside of history, first introduced to me through liberation theology, that opened up other vistas. The patriarchal preoccupation with the winners, and their often violent exploits, drew my attention and curiosity to the losers! After all, those were the ones with whom Jesus stood in solidarity.

The history of religious life too has its winners and losers. Much has been written about the great founders (Anthony, Benedict, Francis, Ignatius), but practically nothing on the great foundresses (Scholastica, Angela Merici, Mary Ward, Mary McKillop). Individual congregations, including my own, lauded their individual achievements, but we were never invited to see the prophetic charismatic power of the vowed life as a global movement. For me, the empowering breakthrough came not by a deeper understanding of my own religious congregation but by the enlarged vision spanning a global context. It was that expansiveness that created the resurrection threshold of my hope and the dream of a more promising future.

It took a few years to embrace that enlarged transpersonal horizon. As often happens when we are blessed with liberating grace, the breakthrough is unexpected and can initially feel daunting and dislocating. It was another stage in my paschal journey.

My Shifting Identity

In the fall of 1987, I was delegated to attend an international meeting in Rome, known in religious life as a general chapter. For some years, I had been growing into a new understanding of my calling, not so much as a priest but as a religious. In conjunction with this shift in my vocational self-understanding, it concerned me greatly that in church law ordination to priesthood was rated more highly than the profession of my final vows. As I understood it, profession of vows involved a commitment to a whole way of life, and particularly a call to live out Gospel values more deeply. Priesthood, on the other hand, felt like one more career, focused on sacramental ministry within a church context.

In the course of the chapter meeting I voiced my concern about this perceived discrepancy and went on to suggest that we should petition the canonical authorities of the Catholic church to reverse the process so that commitment to final vows would take priority over priestly ordination. Despite the fact that none of my colleagues at the meeting showed much enthusiasm for my proposal, I still maintained the sincerity of my convictions.

One of the participants at the meeting, a colleague from Holland, happened to be a canon lawyer. Although he is long dead, I will honor his memory by calling him Johan. Taking me aside, Johan thanked me for making the proposal, assuring me that from a theological perspective, my proposition made an enormous amount of sense. He reminded me, however, that I was asking to change canon law (the official law of the church), and it was highly unlikely that I would ever succeed in doing that. In a more pastoral vein, he reminded me of how easily I could become disillusioned and even embittered pursuing an impossible dream.

Over the next week, Johan and I conversed further about the matter. Thanks to his deep listening and the warmth of his love and reassurance, I reached a place of peace and resolution even before leaving Rome later that month. I began to realize that changing anything substantial in the Catholic church would be an uphill battle, in which, most likely, I would end up consistently as a loser. With my social science knowledge as background, I resolved, therefore, that I would put my energy into changing the world (to whatever extent I could do that) and not invest either my time or my energy in trying to change the church. It probably turned out to be the single greatest decision I ever made, and one I do not regret to this very day.

Over the years, I have been asked more times than I can recall how I manage to survive in the Catholic church, how I manage to reconcile my views with those of the church, how I continue to serve the church while clearly disagreeing with much of its formal teaching. I am never quite sure how to respond to those queries, which seem to be coming from people who are struggling with church issues at a level I am not familiar with. I have never experienced direct conflict with the church, at any level, and I think this is largely due to maintaining my primary commitment to God's world as a Christian social scientist.

From my training in the social sciences, I inherited two great blessings. First, the realization that God works across all times and cultures within an evolutionary unfolding universe, where change is normative for growth and progress. Religions (and churches) are one feature of that cultural landscape, but proportionately, quite a small aspect. Second, the sciences imparted to me a set of discerning skills on how to use creative energy fruitfully and in a way that honors people's deeper needs.

From the church I inherited a faith that was of central importance right into my adult years. The church also provided the central inspiration of my vocation to religious life and gave me the resources I needed to make a difference in the world. I am grateful for all that. I am also grateful, however, for the "hermeneutic of suspicion" that caught up with me in my late twenties, leading to a deep questioning of many inherited truths and a gradual transference from the faith of my childhood to a more mature adult faith. Not surprisingly, adult faith development has become a major dimension of my faith and ministry throughout the latter half of my life.

Seek First the Kingdom

I often think of Johan as the Simon of Cyrene who helped me carry my cross as I was growing into a different vocational identity. With hindsight, I can see I was being called to die to my narrow understanding of church and embrace the call to discipleship in the context of the world. In a short few years that process became all the more congruent as I learned that fidelity to the *kingdom of God* is much more about the world than about the church.

Shortly after my encounter with Johan in Rome, I was asked to facilitate a day's reflection for a group of Anglican clergy in the United Kingdom. The theme for the day was "Living Anew in the Kingdom of God." In the afternoon, one participant thanked me for sharing my wisdom and went on to inform me that he came to the day mainly to see I how would spend an entire day talking about the kingdom of God, a topic on which he found it hard to preach for even ten minutes.

Just a few years previously I might have said exactly the same thing, since my theological formation offered virtually nothing on this central feature of the Gospels. And even though the document *Gaudium et Spes* (The Constitution of the Church in the Modern World) from Vatican II highlighted the fact that the kingdom was bigger and more expansive than the church, that claim made little impact across the worldwide Catholic community.

I built my reflection day around the statement: "But strive first for the kingdom of God and his righteousness, and all these things will be given to you as well" (Matthew 6:33). What was the priority envisaged in this statement, and what did it mean for Christians today? Before engaging that question, I suggested we needed to ask: What did the statement mean for the historical Jesus? Even if some contemporary critical scholars argue that we can't trace the words directly to Jesus (and I am not aware of any who do), even a cursory reading of the Synoptic Gospels verifies beyond doubt that this notion of the kingdom of God was of central importance for Jesus, a fact that has been supported by several scholarly sources throughout the twentieth and twenty-first centuries.[20]

Exploring this foundational aspect of my faith became a major undertaking that engages me—and several adult faith-seekers that I know—until the present time. When we seek to honor the Gospel priority of what many now call "the new reign of God," major adjustments ensue. Even the language itself needs renegotiation. The English word *kingdom*, from the Greek *basileia*, immediately sets us on a deviant course, concerned primarily with imperial power. Other possible translations, based on Hebrew or Aramaic, will give us more direct access to the original oral tradition. My favorite rephrasing—despite its clumsy English feel—is the *companionship of empowerment*.[21] Two central values come to the fore here:

> (a) collaborative empowerment rather than domination from on high, an alternative strategy adopted by Jesus particularly in the parable and miracle narratives; and (b) a strategy of mutual engagement, rather than wisdom from any superior source, as illustrated in the open table fellowship of the Gospels.

From the Personal to the Transpersonal

It is in the establishment of this new empowering companionship that the incarnation of God in Jesus creates a radical new spiritual paradigm. This paradigm is so novel and revolutionary that it has taken Christian scholarship some two thousand years to catch up with its scope. While some scholars seek to locate this new kingdom within the covenantal rule of God in the Hebrew Scriptures, many more consider the New Testament notion of the kingdom as a radical departure not merely from the Hebrew Scriptures but indeed from the divine imperialism discernible in the other great religions as well. Already back in the 1980s, an American scholar, Thomas Sheehan, claimed that Jesus sought to get rid of all formal religion, desiring instead a creation-based spirituality of love and justice in the name of the new reign of God.

The *companionship of empowerment* marks a major shift in our understanding of Christian incarnation. Contrary to most other embodiments of God recorded in the great religions, this new companionship shifts the focus from God's identity with outstanding individual heroes to empowering communities.[22] The new heroism is in the collaborative endeavor to deliver a profound cultural transformation, not merely for humans but for all creation.[23]

Henceforth, all the Christian churches face a major readjustment, a call to move beyond the long-cherished antiworld enclave toward a new way of being present to God's world and its peoples in the form of empowering communities. We got a glimpse of what this would look like in the emergence of the Basic Ecclesial Communities (BEC) movement of Central and South America in the closing decades of the twentieth century. The church at large was not ready for the breakthrough, so the movement was subverted (not crushed as some claim), and will surface again when a more enlightened consciousness will evolve.

Meanwhile, that same empowering communal imperative has exploded around the world and, somewhat similar to the BEC movement, has not received the recognition it deserves. Networking is the systemic strategy best suited to deliver for our twenty-first century the Gospel vision of the companionship of empowerment.

Networking is one of the most inspiring and empowering projects undertaken in the opening years of the present century (as highlighted by the social economist Paul Hawken), and yet has received scant attention in media or in the realms of human discourse. If it were bad news, we would all have heard of it, but, being good news, it is not sensational enough to warrant the attention of newsmakers. Our world is not ready for the empowering liberation of the transpersonal. In this case, we need to die to our lurid fascination with gossip and seductive advertising, so that we can rise to the discerning level of being able to recognize and celebrate movements of our time that promise real hope. And networking is certainly one of those prophetic empowering movements! It is the *companionship of empowerment* flourishing—far beyond the ecclesiastical context to the benefit of our entire creation.

It is the novel relational dimension that seems unique to Christianity, which unintentionally or otherwise seems to have morphed into what came to be known as the doctrine of the Trinity in the fourth century. Long before that doctrine came to be formulated, with its complex metaphysical components, the historical Jesus had pioneered a relational empowering mode of personhood, which our theology has neglected for far too long.

A Person-Centered Faith

Throughout my religious life, I have encountered several allusions to the need for a personal relationship with God (and Jesus) as the basis of every authentic vocation. Here we encounter a Christological horizon that, despite two thousand years of theological development, still requires substantial discerning attention. A dysfunctional anthropology gets in the way, preventing us from evolving from the personal into the transpersonal. The anthropology in question is that of classical Greek times, as developed particularly by Plato and Aristotle. For both of these philosophers, the ensouled creature that can stand over against, and superior to, all other creatures is what constitutes authentic personhood. For Aristotle, the human person is endowed essentially with four characteristics:

Autonomous: ontologically, we each stand independently on our own.[24]

Separate: we are separate from, and superior to, all other aspects of the material creation.

Ensouled: the dimension that links us with God, which no other creature has.

Rational: as ensouled beings we work things out through the God-given power of reason.[25]

It is the subtleties that require closer and more discerning attention. For instance, for many of the Greek fathers (inspired by Aristotle), the *imago Dei* resides in the nonsexual soul, not in the fully embodied human, and much more so in the man than in the woman. And these deviations cannot be explained—as many commentators do—simply by situating Aristotle within the biology and culture of his time. For much of the two thousand years of Christendom, Aristotle tended to be interpreted literally and still enjoys exalted status in scholastic philosophy. This is where things have gone drastically wrong for the appropriation of Christian faith.

It seems to me that Jesus never adopted the Aristotelian understanding of the human person, opting instead for relational becoming rather than the Greek view of the person as a single unified entity, subsistent in its own right, and deemed to be superior to all other earthly creatures. Jesus made a significant shift beyond that appropriation of individualized identity.

For Jesus, personhood is embodied and realized in terms of a relational horizon best encapsulated in the phrase: "I am at all times the sum of my relationships and this is what constitutes my identity." For Jesus, the primary relational matrix is that of the *companionship of empowerment*, understood in the transpersonal realm of all creation (as indicated above). Even Jesus belongs to a reality bigger than the individual person of Jesus himself.

Revisiting the Christian Calling

For much of my early life Jesus was portrayed as a paradigmatic hero, to be emulated and followed. He embodied the fullness of the patriarchal God, as supreme Lord and ruler of the universe. Being a disciple of this God required obedience above all else; that was the supreme virtue. In turn, loyal obedience required childlike trust, not merely in this supreme deity but in all the patriarchal figureheads and institutions allegedly derived from the commands of this ruling God.

Emphasis rested strongly on the fatherhood of God and the church as mother. All disciples (followers), therefore, were to behave like docile, loyal children. It was a parental model, in which the majority of God's people never grew up to become the adult co-disciples envisaged in the companionship of empowerment.

For our time, as we seek to reclaim the new Gospel companionship, the Christian vocation needs to be reenvisioned along these lines: *I do not call you servants but friends, adult co-disciples, serving and earthing the Companionship of Empowerment.* This is the missionary call for all Christians and not merely for those in the "consecrated" state of priesthood or the religious life.

The notion of adult co-disciple is the dimension needing particular attention. Scripture scholars and theologians outline four possible ways of understanding the relationship between the individual Jesus and the kingdom (new companionship):

1. Jesus is equal to the kingdom.
2. Jesus is greater than the kingdom.
3. Jesus is subject to the kingdom.
4. The kingdom can be realized only through the church established in and through Jesus.

Although probably the most controversial, I favor the third option, honoring the relational context of personhood outlined above. Jesus belongs to a reality greater than his individual self and therefore would also include himself in the command that we should seek first the new companionship (Matthew 6:33). Jesus, therefore, may be viewed as the primordial disciple of this new empowering dispensation, with all humans called to be co-disciples—not *for* but *with* Jesus.

As co-disciples we are called to be friends and not mere servants. And there are no privileged power positions in this new dispensation, wherein unconditional love is the primary driving force. Knowing that we are loved unconditionally, then we are called to serve all others—humans and nonhumans alike—with something of that same unconditional love with which we ourselves are loved. Finally, the word *earthing* reminds us unambiguously that it is in and with creation at large that we seek to foster and uphold the power of unconditional love.

Consequently, we should never equate the kingdom of God merely with the life hereafter. The Gospels speak of a future kingdom but also indicate that it is already happening in the here and now, what the scholars describe as realized eschatology. How to reconcile or combine those two time dimensions is a challenge that scholars have never resolved.

Many scripture scholars favor a transformed creation in which the evolutionary imperative could grow and flourish, and humans could enjoy and relish a world in which the meaningless pain and suffering of our time would be considerably reduced. This expansive horizon transcends the long-debated distinctions between a present and future kingdom of God. And we who represent the living Christ today (the body of Christ on earth now) need to err on the side of an expansive and empowering vision, not merely for our own human future (salvation/redemption), but for that of all the other creatures who share the web of life with us. In all probability that is what a contemporary Jesus would want us to do.

I suspect the biggest hurdle for truly understanding Jesus—even to this day—is the enlarged worldview out of which he operated. For Jesus it was all about encountering God in the open space and universality of creation, and not merely in the closed precincts of temple, synagogue, church, or mosque. His vision was neither anti- nor post-religion. It was of an entirely different global ambience.

Dying to Our Imperial Personalism

Christian discernment in every age must wrestle with seeing Jesus in context. For almost two thousand years the context has been that of Western (Roman), white, patriarchal imperialism, within which Jesus was viewed and worshiped as an imperial divine hero. While our distorted spirituality seeks to mold people in the image and likeness of the divine Jesus, we have invested an enormous amount of indoctrination in molding Jesus in our own anthropocentric image and likeness. The classical attributes of the all-powerful, all-knowing, omnipresent God are often projections of our own insatiable hunger for power and domination. We need to die to all this destructive imperial baggage.

What we construed as *personal* was an individualized construct devoid of historical context and molded within a cultural bottleneck capable of choking us to death. For much of Christian history it failed to embrace even the interpersonal so necessary for the mediation and expression of authentic loving. Much more serious is the lack of a planetary and cosmic context that today we understand as essential to what the Jungians call *individuation*, that transpersonal process of becoming that includes the integration of the personal, interpersonal, social, planetary, and cosmic dimensions.

Jesus broke loose from the imperial posturing of his age, providing an alternative anthropology to which most Christians (including scholars) have not yet awakened. It has taken us a long time to transcend the Romanized and Hellenized historical Jesus in favor of what Richard Rohr calls the universal Christ: "Christ is God, and Jesus is Christ's historical manifestation in time.... Instead of saying that God came into the world through Jesus, maybe it would be better to say that Jesus came out of an already Christ-soaked world.... Until we start reading the Jesus story through the collective notion that the Christ offers us, I honestly think we miss much of the core message, and read it all in terms of individual salvation, and individual reward and punishment."[26]

I suggest that those of us in religious life, more than any others, should be highlighting this renewed and revamped Christology. Today, we are a depleted presence with a significantly reduced capacity to influence or inspire. We have lost much of our ecclesiastical glory and cultural influence. Devoid of all the earthly and ecclesiastical attachments of former times can we also let go of the God of patriarchal power that has been undergirding our faith for several centuries?

And as we vowed religious open ourselves to let go of the powerful deity of our past, hopefully we can handle better the diminishment and diminution of this historical moment. In this double letting go, we can actually provide bold prophetic witness by transcending denial, accepting our dying reality, grieve our ending, and die with dignity. In a world where millions die without dignity each day, where we humans maim and massacre millions of indefensible creatures, could anything be more prophetic than showing our world how to handle death with dignity?

In this prophetic endeavor I have been encouraged over many years by the inspiring writings of the scripture scholar Walter Brueggemann. His prophetic admonition will serve as an apt conclusion to the reflections of the present chapter.

> Such rethinking is indeed the work of prophetic imagination that has a calling to walk our society into the crisis where it does not want to go, and to walk our society out of that crisis into an awareness that it does not believe is possible.... Thus I propose that the prophetic community, right in the middle of a culture of denial, is a proper venue for grief work. Such a meeting will not be the happiest place in town. It will only be the most honest place.[27]

CHAPTER FOUR

Dealing with the Sting of Death

Memory is a powerful tool in resisting institutionalized forgetfulness.

—Kwok Pui-Lan

We need to address suffering in a way that gives us a moral imperative to seek its amelioration, not reconcile us with it.

—Elizabeth Johnson

"Where, O death, is your victory? Where, O death, is your sting?" (1 Corinthians 15:55). My first real encounter with the sting of death was in February 1998, when my niece Pauline, eighteen years old, died by suicide. For the immediate family—my brother Pat, his wife Eileen, and their remaining five children—this was a devastating experience that plunged them into a state of numbness where virtually all feeling and emotion were suspended for several months. And those of us in the extended family ruminated in our hearts, wondering if we failed to pick up signals of Pauline's unhappiness and her eventual choice to make this tragic exit from her life on earth.

Pauline had had a difficult adolescence but seemed to be emerging from it. She had arranged to do her driving test the following day. And the few brief notes she left were of little comfort, other than to indicate that for her this felt like the right moment to depart.

As the priest in the family, it was my onerous privilege to deal with the religious ceremonies that, in the Irish context, happen over the few days immediately following death. The funeral Mass is the final event, followed by the burial (or cremation). I have no recollection of how I handled those ceremonies, other than recalling that the words of comfort and consolation I had offered in other funeral contexts were not appropriate. All the words, prayers, readings, and so on felt inadequate. The deep darkness of the occasion was inescapable and deeply painful for our entire family.

A Desperate Search for Meaning

For my psychology degree I had actually done a research project on suicide, reading the relevant literature and interviewing some people who had lost a loved one. My favored resource on the subject was the personal construct theory of the American psychologist George A. Kelly. For Kelly, suicide was a last desperate attempt at meaning in a world that had become meaningless.

Kelly's theory made a great deal of sense in terms of cases I had reviewed during my psychology studies, but when it came to my beloved niece Pauline, all the theories on earth seemed futile. I could not figure out any last desperate attempt in Pauline's life. To the contrary, she seemed to have planned her exit with impeccable precision. My studies also indicated that those contemplating suicide go through deep turmoil but eventually reach a place of inner reconciliation and then carry out their planned exit. That explanation made some sense but did little to alleviate the intense pain all of us in the family were suffering.

Throughout the 1990s, suicide rates in Ireland, particularly among young men in their twenties, grew significantly. Parallels with other European countries were noted, but because of the relatively small population (five million people), the increased incidence in Ireland hit more frequent headlines. Depression and peer pressure were frequently cited causes, but in several cases, causes were impossible to identify. In Pauline's case we learned that she had been friendly with a young man who had taken his life some months previously, and the worry of copycat behavior was also in the air.

There were so many unanswered—and unanswerable—questions. Friends and neighbors were wonderful, but as in many paschal journeys, the deep pain was unassailable, and even the few rational answers available to us did little to ease that pain.

The Healing Power of Ritual

As in all Calvary situations (I am using Christian language here), seedlings of resurrection start to sprout. As a family we were fortunate to identify one that did bring a small measure of comfort and reassurance. It happened a few days after the funeral as I was about to leave and return to London, where I lived at the time. Pauline's older sister suggested that I do a blessing of the shed where she had hanged herself. I talked with the entire family about the matter. They asked that I include some lavender oil in the water (Pauline often used this oil), and we added some salt, a traditional Christian element in water used for ritual blessings.

Together we walked to the shed, entered, and each member of the family sprinkled some of the holy water. For some time we stood in silence and offered a few simple prayers asking for peace and healing. As we returned to the house we sprinkled the entire bowl of water along what we assumed was the final pathway Pauline would have walked on the day of her death.

For myself, that ritual seemed to embody a level of meaning that carried a sense of rightness I had not felt in any of the other ceremonies related to Pauline's death and funeral service. The ritual was to reap benefits that neither I nor any member of the family could have foreseen.

Over the following weeks, each member of the family needed access to that shed; a range of domestic appliances were kept there, as well as clothing for outdoor activities. In every case, the initial apprehension—even the sheer thought of having to go in there—gave way to courageous risk and the experience of a strangely unexpected sense of peace and well-being. Nobody experienced fear or inner turmoil. To the contrary, the building exuded that sense of peace echoed in the oft-cited words of the mystic, Julian of Norwich, "All shall be well and all manner of being shall be well."

Obviously, one cannot provide a logical explanation for the fact that each member of the family experienced that comforting reassurance, but I suspect that the ritual blessing contributed in no small way. The magic of ritual is among the most underestimated and misunderstood dimensions of our lives. Already some seventy thousand years ago our ancient ancestors ritualized the departure and burial of loved ones, adopting a range of symbols loaded with a sense of meaning that cannot be rationally or fully explained either then or now. As human beings we have been ritualizing experiences of our daily lives for longer than records can verify.

Danny's Ritual Breakthrough

Ritual has been a major feature of my life. If I were to choose one example of unique significance it would have to be the story of Danny. In the late 1990s, I worked as a counselor in a project for homeless people in London. Danny, aged twenty-seven at the time, was one of the residents, forever in trouble because of his violent, reactionary behavior. He had been dismissed from several hostels, and in the hope that we could hold on to him (rather than drive him back on to the streets), I, as the resident psychologist, was asked to do some counseling with Danny.

It became quickly apparent that Danny, coming from a highly dysfunctional family and painful background, could not engage in meaningful counseling. It was also abundantly clear that the death of his mother was a major block and probably at the root of many of his other problems.

Danny was only nineteen when his mother died. At that time he was serving a prison sentence and causing many headaches for prison staff as well. Therefore, for his mother's funeral, he was only granted minimal release, chained to two prison guards, and returned to his cell as soon as the burial was complete. It became all too obvious that eight years later, now aged twenty-seven, Danny had not buried his mother, and inviting him to talk about it did not get us very far.

I proposed to Danny that we visit his mother's grave (which he had never done), and I offered to drive him there. Reluctantly he agreed. Both he and I were shocked at the condition of the grave, vastly overgrown with weeds, brambles, and briars. I was not surprised at his angry, emotional reaction expressed in loud shouting, shrieks, and tears. What shocked me was his leaping right into the wild growth as he began rolling around in the midst of the briars and brambles, causing several lacerations all over his face and hands. It took me almost thirty minutes to return him to a sense of calm and bring him back to the hostel. He wept the whole way home.

Over the next week, Danny was very withdrawn, barely eating food, and weeping excessively. He was, however, communicating more openly and turning up for his appointments. There were still occasional aggressive outbursts, but now that the staff were more aware of the background problem, various staff members kept reminding him of the underlying issues around his mother, something that evoked both positive and, at times, negative reactions.

About six weeks later, Danny arrived at one of the counseling sessions carrying a small potted rose bush, which he had purchased without any instigation from me or any staff member, and he asked that I drive him to the graveyard so that he could plant it on his mother's grave. What a moment of breakthrough! Danny was well on the way to burying his mother, after the painful eight years of bottled up grief.

Over the next several months Danny's life changed for the better, with occasional lapses into his old reactionary self. He reached incredible insights into many aspects of his broken dysfunctional past. His mother's grave became a kind of sanctuary that he visited regularly. Twelve months later Danny got a part-time job in a local supermarket and became a permanent employee a few months later. Our resettlement team began the process of transitioning Danny to his own accommodation. Within a few more months, as he approached his thirtieth birthday—and for the first time in his life—he became an adult in his own right. Danny had risen from the dead! Both he and his mother were finally reconciled.

Ritual elevates the human spirit into the transpersonal realm, and as a species we have been doing ritual for several thousand years, long before formal religion ever evolved. Nowhere is this more obvious than the ornate and complex imagery of the Ice Age caves:

> Most painted caves are hard to reach and unfit for human habitation. Entering them is like passing through liminal space, like crossing a threshold between the visible and super-sensible worlds. Some caves show evidence of prolonged activity, and others contain a sort of anteroom where archaeological evidence suggests worshippers may have gathered to eat and

> sleep. But these are not dwelling places; this is sacred space, which explains why the images found inside them are often placed at great distances from the cave's entrance, requiring a perilous journey through labyrinthine passages to view.[28]

For myself and the extended family, Pauline's suicide created a liminal threshold none of us could have crossed without resources that defy ordinary rational understanding. The ritual I describe above was just one of several transpersonal surprises that kept us going over the difficult weeks and months that followed. As every anniversary came round we gathered and gave thanks for her life. Unknown to ourselves, we were also giving thanks for the healing that time made possible, a journey toward wholeness that every pilgrim knows.

From the Personal to the Transpersonal

Throughout the human family death carries a sense of dread and oblivion, a human plight that we hope can one day be conquered and eliminated. Such a negative view of death has been consistently reinforced by the Christian narrative of Christ's own death marking the beginning of the end of death and dying. A complex sacrificial rhetoric underpins the Christian paschal mystery. Jesus is the final sacrificial lamb capable of placating an angry (or loving) God, making up once and for all for the sins of humanity, which allegedly caused the curse of death in the first place. And while the death (and resurrection) of Jesus initiates the undoing of the curse of death, even Christianity itself has frequently doled out deadly violence in seeking to undermine and defeat its enemies.

This inherited narrative, which becomes ever more unbelievable with the passing of time, deals exclusively with human beings in a perverse anthropology that also has lost much credibility in our time. Only humans matter. They are the ones who sinned, creating a universal contagion that affects even creation at large. The entire creation is reduced to human fickleness.

In the transpersonal approach we seek to honor the primacy of creation itself, and resituate the human within that context. Death and the possibility of new life (resurrection in Christian terms) belong first and foremost to creation, and without properly understanding that foundational context then we end up with gross distortions of the type that underpin the theories of atonement in both Judaism and Christianity. So, let's get clarity on the transpersonal dimensions and then reframe the personal context.

The paschal journey features in every aspect of God's creation. It is usually described as the paradox of *creation-cum-destruction* (with both concepts carrying equal weight), otherwise named as *the unfolding cycle of birth-death-rebirth*. And it transpires all over creation, on the macro and micro scales alike. At both the cosmic and planetary levels we witness this enduring paradoxical mix of newness bursting forth only to yield in due course to decline, fragmentation, and termination.[29] "In the deep space," writes Michio Kaku, "we must face the reality that most of the universe is in turmoil, with lethal radiation belts and swarms of deadly meteors."[30]

At the galactic level, a supernova marks the death of a star. When a massive star runs out of fuel, it cools off. This causes the pressure to drop. Gravity wins out, and the star suddenly collapses. The collapse happens so quickly that it creates enormous shock waves that cause the outer part of the star to explode! That resulting explosion is a supernova. And from that explosion we receive the fundamental building blocks of the universe that form the core of most stars: hydrogen, helium, carbon. At the cosmic and local level alike, the death of the star marks a resurrection to new life, the ubiquitous paschal journey.

Is this how God created the world? It seems so—to which the average religionist is likely to retort: "How could anyone believe in such a capricious God?" But who is actually capricious, God or us? Many of us have been heavily indoctrinated by the classical Greek notion of the perfect, omniscient (all-knowing), omnipotent (all-powerful), transcendent (totally independent of all else), immutable (never changing), impassible (beyond suffering), eternal God, the one who rules and controls everything. Most people don't seem to realize that these divine attributes are actually *projections* of a human species seeking absolute control over everything. The all-powerful deity is actually a projection of power-hungry humans. Such an understanding of God is little more than five thousand years old and is significantly different from how we related with Holy Mystery for most of our evolutionary story of some seven million years.

Our ancient ancestors had a very different understanding of the divine life force. Because of their closeness to the natural world, the ancients, somewhat like contemporary indigenous (tribal) peoples, knew a convivial relationship with the living universe, experiencing the daily interaction of life and death, creation and destruction, without—it seems—our contemporary compulsion for domination and control. What to many of our contemporaries seems like a baffling paradox (creation-cum-destruction) was known to our ancestors for thousands of years before Greek metaphysics and patriarchal domination wrecked the whole perceptual edifice. And this earth-centered affiliation was not some type of infantile enmeshment, as the Greeks suggested. It was a quality of engagement, the deeper meaning of which seems to have eluded the patriarchal worldview of recent millennia.

Engaging the Power of Paradox

The key word here is *paradox*, which may be described as "a contradiction with meaning written underneath." On the surface, it makes little or no sense. Only the discerning eye (or heart) can perceive the underlying meaning. A familiar example occurs in the writings of St. Paul: "When I am weak then I am strong" (2 Corinthians 12:9–11). At a rational level, the statement makes no sense, yet many among us can recall experiences within which the statement rings true. It is the mystic more than anybody else that can entertain and embrace this paradoxical wisdom.

This alternative consciousness, with its capacity for deeper perception and understanding, is not merely a feature of human life but an evolutionary endowment that characterizes all creation at the cosmic and planetary levels alike. Birth and death are not merely human experiences; they characterize the whole of God's creation. On the planetary scale, earthquakes serve as a good example. Metaphorically, an earthquake can be described as the earth-body releasing its pent-up energies, so that it can continue to grow and flourish in a more creative way. Without earthquakes, we would have no earth, nor would any of us be around even to speculate on this baffling paradox of birth-death-rebirth.

So, does God will the death of 240,000 innocent people, as happened in Pakistan in 2005, or of wholesale environmental catastrophe resulting from the 2004 Indian Ocean tsunami? There is no logical or rational answer to this question because we are engaging a form of wisdom that is beyond rationality. Worthy of note, however, is the fact at an 8.0 earthquake (Richter scale) in the island of Guam in 1991 resulted in no human casualties, while that of Pakistan (7.4 on the Richter scale) led to 240,000 deaths. When we note that the island of Guam is a colony of the United States, with all earthquake-resistant buildings, and that Pakistan is a country too poor to afford such structures, we begin to see a way through the paradox. It quickly becomes obvious that the problem is not with the earthquake, nor with God, but with the avaricious humans who choose not to share resources equally and justly across the human population.

We knew how to cope with an earthquake in Guam. We could do so universally if we were committed to justice and equality all around. In terms of the paschal journey, here we confront its challenge head on: Can we, patriarchal humans, addicted to domination and control, die to (let go of) our power compulsion, so that we can be raised to a more egalitarian, mutually empowering way of being, for our own benefit and that of all creation?

Admittedly, we cannot always find a meaningful or reasonable explanation for those freaks of nature that wreak havoc on nonhuman life-forms. When dealing with paradox there will always be untidy elements that transcend rational explanation.

But even in such situations we need to press the human dimension. Look at Hurricane Katrina in New Orleans in 2005 and superstorm Sandy along the east coast of the United States in October 2012. Nothing to do with humans, we are quick to retort! A capricious act of God, others suggest! In the wake of Katrina commentators noted that hurricanes seem to come with a much greater ferocity than previously recorded. Other environmentally related factors, such as global warming, may be a contributory factor, which immediately raises suspicion of a human contribution as we slowly but gradually realize that indirect human interference, reinforcing a range of ecological imbalances, may well be a critical factor in several major natural catastrophes.

While we cannot be certain about the human role in natural catastrophes, it is becoming increasingly clear that human behavior contributes significantly to many forms of meaningless suffering on our earth. In recent times this has struck home with the devastating impact of the coronavirus in 2020. The evil we seek to impute elsewhere—to Satan or the devil—may well be a deluded projection that arises from our own wrong interference in the scheme of things, our inability to step back and respect nature's own paradoxical ways. At the very least we need to come to terms with our appalling ignorance of the paradoxical world we inhabit. Only when we become aware of the great paradox will we gradually begin to realize that most of the meaningless suffering within and around us is actually caused by humans, not by God or by natural catastrophes. It is our ignorance of the great paradox, and our inability (or unwillingness) to engage it proactively, that is at the root of most if not all the meaningless suffering in the world.

The Meaning of Suffering

The perennial question, therefore, relates to the suffering we humans cause and exacerbate, because apparently we have lacked the wisdom to read the great paradoxes of life in a more enlightened way. A universe without pain and suffering is simply impossible. Suffering in itself is endemic to every evolutionary breakthrough, desired by our creative God. Suffering is not the problem; it is our faulty perceptions that cause the problem. It is we who need to change, not the messy world that has been messed up in the first place by our reckless interference. The British philosopher Terry Eagleton captures well the underlying confusion when he writes: "There is a diabolic delight to be reaped from the notion of absolute destruction. Flaws, loose ends, and rough approximations are what evil cannot endure. This is one reason why it has a natural affinity with the bureaucratic mind. Goodness, by contrast, is in love with the dappled, unfinished nature of things."[31]

Eagleton goes on to make a second crucial observation about the meaningless suffering that surrounds us on a daily basis. Contrary to the claim that the fundamental flaw of original sin is a major contributory factor, Eagleton writes: "The point is that most wickedness is institutional. It is the result of vested interests and anonymous processes, not of the malign acts of individuals."[32] To which I would like to add: It is the corruption and usurpation of power within all of our major institutions that cause most, if not all, the meaningless suffering in the modern world. It is when we cannot see, or don't wish to see, the need to step back from (die unto) our irrational need for domination and control that we contribute most to the meaningless suffering in the world.

The insidious nature of human angst and misery is partly due to the Christian notion of atonement. The doctrine was invented to once more reinforce human control, employing the leading ideology of feudal times. First introduced in the Middle Ages, mainly by St. Anselm, the basic argument goes like this: God was angry with humankind's waywardness (sin), and, like a feudal lord, God demanded that satisfaction and reparation should be made. And he chose (or persuaded) his son, Jesus, to be the necessary scapegoat. Jesus paid the penalty of humanity's sin, bringing forgiveness, imputing righteousness, and reconciling us all to God.

According to this view, Jesus's death paid the penalty for sin, and through our faith we can now accept Christ's substitution as payment for all human sinning. Another deluded dream of power-mongering humans, once again oblivious of the paschal nature of life, the letting-go, so essential to the cosmic letting be(coming).

In the closing decades of the twentieth century, several Christian scholars highlighted the flawed nature of atonement theory itself. The French theorist Rene Girard claims that penal substitution is an inherently *violent* model of the atonement and has achieved little other than reinforcing the very violence it seeks to eradicate. Several feminist theologians view atonement theory as a form of "divine child abuse," one that has contributed significantly to the victimization of women in particular. Black liberation theologian James Cone links the model to defenses of slavery and colonialism, while British ethicist Michael Northcott suggests that it is no coincidence that leaders of the Religious Right, for whom the model is so central, are such staunch advocates of the *lex talionis*, capital punishment, and the war on terror.

In the light of these reflections, it seems grossly irresponsible to lump together *human sin*, *death*, and *Satan*. Death is an integral dimension of all organic life-forms. Death is a God-given endowment, without which we cannot have new life. Death is not an evil to get rid of but a central ingredient of the life force that needs to be understood in another light. We must stop demonizing death and instead learn to befriend it responsibly.

The Denial of Death

After evil and suffering, death is the next great enemy we would love to conquer. For St. Paul, death is the consequence of sin (Romans 6:23); it entered the world through the deviant behavior of the original human, Adam (Romans 5:12). For St. Paul, and subsequent generations of Christians, the death and resurrection of Jesus has "destroyed death forever" (1 Corinthians 15:26), and to that utopian hope millions of Christians still adhere.

The great Eastern religions of Hinduism and Buddhism take a very different approach, viewing death in reincarnational terms, whereby life and death are interwoven in an evolving recurring cycle, culminating in the release of the soul into the eventual fulfillment of Nirvana.

Most humans in the contemporary world dread death to the point where most of us refuse even to think about it, until life's circumstances compel us to do so, and then we either seek to escape the challenge or rationalize it as far as possible. Despite this widespread fear, we rub shoulders with death on a daily basis and remain largely unaffected by the deadly termination of life we mete out to fellow humans and to so many other species of our earth.

Our passive acceptance of the endless media coverage of carnage and atrocity betrays a love-hate relationship with death. We are simultaneously repelled by its terror and seduced by its mystique. The popular appeal of violent video games and Hollywood horror movies provides further proof of our morbid fascination with death. The overexposure to images and messages of death seems to have desensitized us to the terror of meaningless death and has made us more tolerant of violence and the random destruction of several life-forms.

We need a radical reconstruction of death and its universal meaning. To that end I make the following key points:

1. Death is an integral dimension of the great paradox of creation-cum-destruction, the recurring cyclic process of birth-death-rebirth, outlined in this chapter. If we get rid of death, we have immediately terminated life as well.

2. Death cannot be properly understood without a deeply integrated awareness and internalization of the great paradox described above, the foundational outline of the paschal journey understood in universal terms.

3. Death is not a limitation or an evil in any sense. Death is a necessary good, an evolutionary, God-given imperative for the development and flourishing of all life-forms.

4. The negative preoccupation with death is largely the product of imperial patriarchal consciousness, the insatiable desire to conquer and control all life forces, to the deluded advantage of the patriarchs themselves.

5. Monotheistic religions, heavily influenced by the patriarchal value system, reinforce the negative and problematic dimensions of death.

6. The violent glamorization of death in public media is a perverse defense mechanism against the self-induced horror of death. We will need to clear away this perverse rubble before rehabilitating death in a more integrated way.

7. Despite all the utopian hope of the various religions, most humans do not die with dignity or with responsible love and care. Millions each year die anonymously and are not given a proper burial.

8. Theologian Elizabeth Johnson draws an important distinction between personal death and social death, describing personal death as a biological reality that must be maturely integrated, and social death as a disaster we must ethically resist.

The Cross and Resurrection of Jesus

In the last chapter, we outlined the liberating and empowering mission of Jesus encapsulated in the notion of the companionship of empowerment (my suggested renaming for the kingdom of God). To this dream Jesus gave everything, *primarily in his life*, lived to such a depth of commitment that it cost him his earthly life. Because he was empowering so many people not merely by preaching and teaching but primarily through healing and the practice of the open, inclusive table, the forces of imperial domination (Roman and Jewish) felt enormously threatened, to a point where they could tolerate his presence no longer. They set out to trap him, and eventually did so, in the dark of night (when his followers could not safeguard him). According to some scholars, he was crucified and had died before any of his followers or family knew about it. Because the Gospels were written decades after the events they describe, details may have been added by the authors for theological reasons.

His death was quick, brutal, and vindictive, completely devoid of any human or sacred meaning. He did not choose to die, nor did he die for our sins. He was killed by crucifixion, the death penalty specially selected for subversives who posed a threat to the Roman imperial system.

Christians have long considered the cross to be the primary symbol of divine deliverance and of God's ultimate loving sacrifice for humanity. For St. Paul, there is only one Gospel, that of the death and resurrection of Jesus. Some scripture scholars in the late 1800s claimed that this is the central feature of the Gospels, and all the other material about the life of Jesus is merely a preface for that which is really important.

From a transpersonal perspective, I opt for the opposite interpretation. It is the *life* of Jesus that is all important, particularly the cosmic empowering dispensation of the kingdom of God. *The death is a very small part,* the consequence of a life fully and radically lived. To highlight, glamorize, and celebrate such a cruel, barbaric event verges on blasphemy. This is the reckless patriarchal violence that every authentic religion should be denouncing and renouncing. Without such a rejection, religion will continue to stand accused of fomenting the violence and abuse that continues to wreak havoc on our world even to this day.

With these sentiments one is often accused of dodging the issue to suffering so prevalent in our world. I acknowledge that Jesus suffered, sometimes intensely, in his life (and not merely in his death) in order to rid the world of meaningless suffering. And let's be crystal clear also about the fact that Jesus never advocated suffering for its own sake. The goal of his life and mission was to *rid the world of all meaningless suffering.*

The horror, violence, and injustice of his untimely death are often misconstrued because of how Christians throughout the ages have understood that event/experience known as the resurrection. In its literal understanding, Jesus, unknown to anybody, and without any human assistance, came out of the grave and had bodily encounters with the apostles and others before ascending back to the heavenly realm outside this earth. Volumes have been written on this topic, long understood to be the greatest miracle of all, in which Jesus himself overcame death and rose from the grave in a newly constituted body. In this approach, death and resurrection always go together.

Throughout the second half of the twentieth century, Christian scholars raised doubts about this literal interpretation. For one thing the three-tier cosmology makes no sense in our time. And when it comes to the resurrection appearances recorded in the Gospels, we need to remember the cultural context where spirit-power was very real, and people had the capacity for mystical/visionary experiences long lost to our contemporaries. Recall the cryptic reminder from John Dominic Crossan: "My point, once again, is not that those ancient people told literal stories and we are now smart enough to take them symbolically, but that they told them symbolically and we are now dumb enough to take them literally."[33] The Gospel encounters with the risen Jesus may be more indicative of what was happening to the followers than of what happened to Jesus himself. Literalists in the past used the empty tomb as "proof" for the resurrection of Jesus, but those that continued to follow Jesus based their faith not on the evidence of an empty tomb but rather on the new awakening of God's living Spirit in their midst.

In other words, the power of the resurrection is better discerned through the transformation wrought in the disillusioned followers of Jesus in the weeks and months after his tragic death, rather than in what may have happened to Jesus himself. Instead of speculating on what actually happened to Jesus, let's ask, "What was the transformative power whereby the shattered, disillusioned disciples came back to a quality of faith on which they staked everything from thereon, even to the point of a martyr's death?"[34]

This links resurrection with life rather than with death. It then becomes what Christian theology frequently asserts: "the fullness of life." In that case, resurrection can be viewed as God's ultimate vindication that the life of Jesus (and not so much his death) was a life dedicated to transformative empowerment and extensive liberation.

Quantum physics helps to deepen our understanding of resurrection (as explained above) while also illuminating the mystery of death—our own and that of the historical Jesus. All life-forms are constituted and sustained by living energy, that same life force that enlivens everything in the creation around us. And it seems that energy needs to be embodied to function and flourish; without body, energy cannot do much. In the experience of my death—whatever the cause—the energy departs from my particular embodied configuration but does not evaporate into nothing. According to the basic laws of physics, energy is never wasted. Energy always reconnects with energy, to seek out a new embodied articulation, which is another way of understanding the enlivening power of resurrection energy after the death of Jesus.

After my death, the energy of my embodied existence will go elsewhere. Exactly where, I don't know, and why do I need to know? Why not trust the universal cosmic wisdom within which energy is always recycled to co-create even more complex organisms, human and otherwise? This is a reckless sense of trust in the benevolent nature of the universe—what Christians might call *resurrection hope!*

What I postulate in this explanation need not be in conflict with belief in an afterlife of heaven or hell. Rather, it confronts us with the likelihood that we make our own heaven or hell, not in some distant transcendent realm but right here in front of our eyes. The thousands of innocent children who die prematurely every day is hell on earth, and so is the butchery that results from warfare and violence. It is the pseudo-transcendence we attach to death that makes it so tragic and frequently meaningless. We need to resolve the dilemma of death, not in some transcendent afterlife or by projecting on to a divine scapegoat on a cross, but right here upon the earth itself.

Befriending the Great Paradox

The language of paradox is written all over creation. It is there for us to read and discern. When we do attend to it, it seems to make life more tolerable, more bearable; dare I suggest, more meaningful. When we fail to attend, we expose ourselves to forces that can be cruel and devastating. Apparently, we do have a choice. The big problem, however, is that the choice seems to lead in directions that are alien to our imperial Western consciousness, to our rational ways of perceiving and acting, to our prized sense of being in control of the contingent nature of the world we inhabit. To opt for the other choice feels like betraying or abandoning all we have worked so hard for, all that constitutes the very foundations of a civilized world.

And for many Christians, diminishing the central role of the death and resurrection of Jesus leaves them vulnerable and confused. Without the comfort and consolation of the cross, without the divine power of resurrection, promising to destroy death forever, what's the point of believing in Jesus or the Christian way? The point, of course, is that Jesus did not set out to destroy death, which would mean destroying a central dynamic of all creation. Instead through both his life and death, he confronted the meaningless death we humans recklessly and thoughtlessly pursue and challenged us to change our ways.

When we give our lives for the sake of empowerment of the other, we embrace the paradox that is central to every paschal journey. This is not death pursued for its own sake, nor is it suffering for the sake of suffering. It is the daily cross we are all asked to undertake to rid our world of the meaningless suffering largely caused by the blindness that is unable to see the enduring paradox on which all life flourishes.

Whether we engage the paradox on the grand cosmic scale or consider its application to our individual lives, the challenge is equally daunting. The first hurdle we need to negotiate is the persistent indoctrination of dualistic splitting, dividing life into the binary opposites of earth versus heaven, matter versus spirit, body versus soul. The illumination of truth does not belong to the clarity of the polar opposites but to the gray area in between, where, day in and day out, we work out the meaning of life.

This is where the real stuff happens. Here is where we encounter afresh our inherited patriarchal, dualistic, and imperialistic wisdom and face the disturbing truth that deeper meaning evolves elsewhere—in the restless, pulsating throes of an evolving universe ever inviting us to new horizons, ever risky, yet persistently creative!

CHAPTER FIVE

Beyond Patriarchal Insularism

> *Questioning of our religious belonging and attempts to discover a more benevolent view of God often bring the spiritual pilgrim to inner conflict. Standing between two or more worlds, many souls suffer an impasse between religious worldviews. Unable to go back to who and what we once were, but uncertain about how to enter the future, feelings of confusion, betrayal, disinterest, and anguish are not uncommon. In fact, many people confide the pain of their alienation from traditional religious norms. As an essential aspect of healing, this process of impasse and anguish is a mark of the substance and authenticity of the path. When the self is pushed against darkness and unknowing, the impasse itself becomes a catalyst for a more honest understanding of reality.*
>
> —Beverly Lanzetta

My dad was born in 1900 and could remember well the First World War (1914–1918). Etched more vividly in his imagination, however, was the Irish Civil War (1922–1923). He often pointed out to me the missing bark from the big sycamore tree in front of our house, an erasure he claimed was made by bullets from an Irish Republican Army (IRA) gun.

My dad would proudly consider himself a staunch republican with an undeniable hatred for Britain, and all things British, despite the fact that four of his siblings emigrated to the United Kingdom, worked and reared families there, and did well for themselves. As a child and teenager, I internalized much of his patriotic zeal, and as a teenager in 1966, celebrating the fiftieth anniversary of the Easter Rising of 1916, I proudly raised our national flag each day at the school where I was studying.

I too harbored that deep resentment toward all things British, including the Protestant religion, which I considered to be synonymous with that culture. Perhaps it was for that reason that the provincial superior of my religious order sent me to work in England immediately after my ordination to priesthood. It turned out to be a transformative experience, leaving an indelible mark on my psyche for many years to come.

Shortly after arriving in the United Kingdom in 1974, I went to visit some relations in London. As I walked along Oxford St., in central London, I saw two black men walking toward me. I quickly moved to the opposite footpath to avoid what felt like a dangerous threat. It was my racist prejudice instigating my irrational fear. I walked around Hyde Park (also in central London), mesmerized and thrilled to see so many nuns in habits walking around. Two years later, as I overcame my cultural ignorance, I came to realize that they were not nuns at all; they were Muslim women.

The Cultural Shift

Several other cultural adjustments happened that year. Yet nothing could have prepared me for the baptism of fire that was to ensue about six months after my arrival in the United Kingdom. In my home country of Ireland, violence had erupted in Northern Ireland (still under British jurisdiction). It was partly a war between Catholics and

Protestants that morphed into a more deadly encounter between a dissident group known as the IRA (Irish Republican Army) and the British military. Many lives were lost on both sides before, fortunately, a peaceful resolution, known as the Good Friday Agreement, was negotiated in April 1998.

Back in 1974, I was traveling by train to visit relatives in Bristol. It was a Friday evening, and the train was well full. I found a table seat, with vacant seats across from me. A few moments later those seats were occupied by two British soldiers in full military uniform. I could feel the rage rising up inside me and looked around for a vacant seat, but none was available. All I could do was sit it out and hope for the best.

They tried to engage me in conversation, and, reluctantly, I agreed. They informed me that they were on their way to Northern Ireland on military duty. It was their first overseas assignment. One of the men was twenty years old and the other twenty-one. Having detected my Irish accent they asked several questions about Ireland, which I tried to answer civilly, always conscious of the strong resentment going on deep inside me. Over the course of the journey I mellowed considerably as they offered me some of their food, chocolates, and even cigarettes (smoking on public transport was allowed then).

Two and a half hours later, having arrived in Bristol, I myself was baffled at how much I had come to like these two guys. As we disembarked the train, we exchanged warm handshakes, and I wished them well for their time in Northern Ireland.

The following Tuesday, on the front pages of leading British newspapers were photographs of the same two same guys—shot dead by the IRA in Northern Ireland. Not only was I in shock and disgust, I could feel a rage within me the likes of which I had never before experienced. That whole day I was like a zombie, emotionally and psychologically devastated. I was being dragged into one of the biggest conversions I would ever undergo.

Everything on which I had staked my life and meaning—my Irish republicanism, my hatred of the British, my Catholic superiority, my internalization of imperial victimization—was unraveling in front of my eyes. It was like being stripped naked of all I felt comfortable within. For me, Ireland would never be the same again.

The Ecumenical Challenge

Later that year, I had an opportunity to visit Taizé in France. Located there was the international, ecumenical religious community about which I had read so much and seemed to be offering a new way for living monastic life in particular, as well as religious life at large. The trip was organized by the British branch of the United Society for the Propagation of the Gospel, and most members of the group were Protestant. Traveling by coach through France on a Sunday, we stopped for refreshments, and during that break, the group leader, an Anglican priest, suggested we would celebrate a simple Eucharist. Laying out a cloth on the grass, using some ordinary bread and wine, he proceeded to lead us in the celebration.

Knowing me to be a priest as well, and apparently the only other clergyman in the group, he issued an invitation for me to concelebrate with him (if I so wished). I promptly declined. Everything about that experience of Eucharist evoked horror for me and a deep sense of guilt that I was even participating in the charade. Yet, when the bread and wine were passed around, I took and received the same as everybody else. Why I participated made no logical or rational sense, and it took quite a few years to accept the rightness of what transpired at that Eucharist.

What made the experience even more bewildering was the young woman in the group, who somehow knew I was Catholic and came to me afterward, expressing her puzzlement that I, a Catholic, participated in a Protestant Eucharist. I have no recollection what response I made, but I do recall a further sense of guilt that I might have unduly disturbed her conscience by the bad example I was giving.

Many years later, the double experience began to make sense. So dislocating was the first experience, a radical dying to my Irish nationalism, a Calvary that destroyed so much of what seemed sacrosanct in my early life, that the participation in the Protestant Eucharist carried a certain logicality. It was a further stage in the dying to my inherited sectarian Catholicism. The Calvary breakthrough had already commenced before I left Taizé a week later. From here on ecumenism was not merely a lofty theological idea; it was to become a major thrust in the future development of my Christian faith.

And it would go far beyond Christianity. Within a short number of years, I had visited worship centers of all the major world religions and participated in several of their liturgies. I began to appreciate the complex richness of the various religions, but I also began to understand how each religion represents a historical period in which patriarchal values were very much to the fore. Beneath and behind all the major religions was a more ancient deeper spiritual significance. Such spirituality became the foundation for a lifelong endeavor, an exploration that continues to the present time.

The resurrection breakthrough from that double Calvary of many previous years continues to engage, challenge, and inspire me, and I believe it will for the rest of my life. Some dimensions of the paschal journey have impacted me on a more short-term basis, but the spiritual horizon of humanity and our world is indeed ever old and ever new.

From the Personal to the Transpersonal

The sturdy foundations of my inherited Catholic upbringing were shaken to the core by the end of 1974, living in the United Kingdom. And perhaps destiny was at work, because a few years later I would return to the United Kingdom and live there for the next thirty years of my life, a time of great personal fruitfulness marked by the expansion of several of my life's horizons.

My faith horizon expanded from my sectarian Catholicism into the ecumenical sphere of the other Christian denominations, only to realize that in several ways they were as sectarian and narrow as my own denomination. And the multicultural nature of Britain opened up the possibility for a range of encounters with other world religions, notably Hinduism, Buddhism, and, on a smaller scale, Sikhism. My experience of Islam at that time was not very wholesome, as I encountered sectarian elements much more entrenched than I had ever experienced in my traditional Catholic upbringing.

Sometime in the 1980s in the United States, I met the first people who had journeyed through a number of faith commitments, starting, perhaps, with a shift from one Christian denomination to another, going through periods of agnosticism, and possibly a multifaith engagement with something like Buddhist meditation. Many of these struck me as quite wholesome people, who were not randomly experimenting but rather engaging a pilgrim journey of a strong mystical flavor. Not until the opening years of the twenty-first century did I discover more formal research on this phenomenon, under the rubric of comparative theology or multiple religious belonging.

Meanwhile my own faith journey had evolved in another direction. Beneath all the denominations and religions, and sometimes in the lives of people describing themselves as atheist or agnostic, I began to discern a deeper strand, which I and others have named as spirituality. That continues to engage my spirit and my imagination.

Until my early twenties, my Irish nationalism and Catholic identity were effectively one and the same. I had internalized a strong sense of belonging to the "Island of Saints and Scholars." My people took an inordinate pride in our religious distinctiveness. We had it right to a degree that no other nation had, and, through our missionaries, we were privileged to bring the light of pure truth to the pagan nations of the world. As far as we Irish were concerned, every other nation on earth was pagan to one degree or another. And the most pagan of them all was England. The people of Britain had been and continued to be our oppressors. We labeled all the Brits as Protestants, and for us that religion was the epitome of pure evil. Even to stand inside a Protestant church was seriously sinful. To participate in any kind of non-Catholic service was an unforgivable sin.

I realize now that for much of my early life I had imbibed a manipulative idolatry rather than a liberating religion. Light and shadow intermingle in every sphere of our lives, and religion is not immune. The very notion of religious worship involves walking a tightrope between adult maturation and childish (fearful) dependency. Holding truth lightly can be healthier than excessive zeal. We have much to learn from those indigenous First Nations peoples who do not employ the notion of worship. Instead ritual engagement is viewed as befriending the God(s), or facilitating the possibility of being befriended by God, rather than submitting in terms of conventional loyal obedience to some kind of a heavenly superpower.

Throughout much of our long prehistoric story, we humans lived within the culture of a spiritual allurement. We can certainly trace evidence for this to ancient burial rites that possibly date to 150,000 years ago. Obviously we are dealing with much more substantial evidence in the vast global repertoire of Ice Age art, conservatively dated to forty thousand years ago. Noteworthy in this ancient spiritual tradition is a diverse, amorphous notion of God. Polytheism rather than monotheism was the norm. The multiple understandings of the deity in those earlier times did not involve the notion of submissive worship that becomes a central feature of mainline religion as we have known it for the past five thousand years.

In my upbringing, there were only two religions, Catholic and Protestant, one totally right and the other an abomination beyond words. Even my theological training did little to open me up to other world religions. Hinduism and Buddhism were merely words describing some strange pagan allegiance that was none of our business. And in case the reader thinks I am adopting a somewhat extreme position, I wish to recall the painfully sad events of the 1990s when multifaith theologians such as Jacques Dupuis, Roger Haight, and Michael Amaladoss were severely reprimanded by Rome for promoting what today we call comparative theology. The religious ideology of my childhood and adolescent years lasted longer than many of us would wish.

Enter Monotheism

As far as I can recall, my theological formation in the early 1970s never distinguished between monotheism and polytheism. Every understanding of God, different from our Christian Jesus, was wrong—plain and simple! There was only one true God and that was Jesus, and the role of the church was to teach and protect that one authentic truth.

For many spiritual people of our time this is a landscape so muddled and confused that millions are simply walking away, preferring to separate completely from it rather than trying to understand it. To them monotheism feels like a primitive ideology best forgotten and consigned to the archives of history. Our evolutionary context throws a different light on things. At every level of life, evolution requires us to forego the old in favor of the new, a novel perspective evoked by the lure of the future rather than based on allegiance to the past.

There are undercurrents to the notion of monotheism that have rarely been named and therefore scarcely never addressed. As a concept, monotheism first becomes a preoccupation in the emergence of Judaism around 1000 BCE. The context is local, tribal, and insinuated with a patriarchal drive for dominance and control.[35] It is based on an unquestioned presupposition—which is in fact a patriarchal projection—that God is a human-like king, ruling from above the sky, the creator of the whole world and the only primary source to whom we owe full allegiance.

How and why the Jewish people came to this unquestionable conclusion is difficult to assess, because a vast range of diverse understandings of God, and God's relationship to the world, prevailed across several ancient cultures. Polytheism rather than monotheism was the norm, with this notable addendum; however, that within and beneath the great religious diversity, a sense of God's oneness was widely adopted, particularly within the great mystical traditions. As I shall indicate later, this sense of oneness is a relational rather than a metaphysical notion, and many religious problems, right down to our own day, can be traced to this misunderstanding.

Monotheism therefore includes an implicit declaration that in heaven there is only one source of authentic power, and from that one source, authentic earthly powers draw their validation. Furthermore, there is an implicit anthropology, claiming that the ruling God is a human-like creature and concerned largely (if not solely) with human beings. The welfare and salvation of other creatures, and of creation at large, is of little concern to this monotheistic God.

The God of Genesis 1 is a God of all creation, and creation is the context for engagement and revelation. The Old Testament (Hebrew Scriptures) quickly loses sight of that panoramic view, as warring humans become the major preoccupation throughout the rest of the Old Testament. The egalitarian relationship with the web of life gets congealed into human wrangling over power and domination. Even God becomes insinuated into the violent foray, frequently supporting the victorious winner, who then seeks exclusive domination in the name of an exclusive monotheistic God.

Monotheism and the Unifying Power of Spirit

Monotheism has long been considered an advanced, sophisticated mode of engagement when compared with the primitive tenor of earlier cultural norms. Here we encounter several unexamined assumptions.

The emergence of formal religion follows quite closely other evolutionary developments of the past ten to twelve thousand years, beginning with the agricultural revolution around 10,000 BCE. Prior to that time, the evidence points toward a human species who coexisted in a convivial way with the living earth itself, perceived to be energized by the organic spirit of God, probably along lines similar to indigenous peoples in the contemporary world. Central to that ancient spirituality was the notion of the divine as the Great Spirit, understood to be embodied primarily not in some distant heaven but within the organicity of the living earth itself. How the people engaged with the Great Spirit can be gleaned from a third-century inscription found in the city of Oenoanda in Southwest Asia Minor (modern Turkey):

> Born of itself, untaught, without a mother, unshakeable, not contained in a name known by many names, dwelling in fire, this is God. We, his angels, are a small part of God. To you

> who ask this question about God, what his essential nature is, he has pronounced that Aether is God who sees all, on whom you should gaze and pray at dawn, looking to the sunrise.[36]

Long before the evolution of formal religion as we know it today—beginning with Hinduism around 3000 BCE—humans engaged with spiritual meaning across a vast range of understandings and experiences. We cannot and must not identify this vast diversity with polytheism, which in its literal meaning denotes the worship of several gods, rather than the one true deity. As already indicated there is a unifying factor, namely, God as spirit, and that spiritual lifeforce is experienced at a range of different levels. There is, however, one core dimension to that multifaceted experience, namely, the surrounding creation. Therein, more than anywhere else, our ancient ancestors encounter the vitality of the living Spirit.

There is a unity within the diversity, but it has nothing to do with the later understanding of monotheism. The earlier ancient experience was transpersonal, rather than personal, in the sense of prioritizing humans. The encounter with the Great Spirit happened first and foremost in and through the created universe. Contrary to the monotheistic approach, the Great Spirit was experienced not as a transcendent power on which all was dependent, but rather as a convivial life force, with which humans were invited to co-create. In several cases, the invitation to such co-creation happened through ritual engagement.

Most important of all is the issue of power and empowerment. The monotheistic God is one of unilateral power, who alone can save humans from the plight of their sinfulness. The notion of salvation is largely absent from faith in the Great Spirit. Trust in the benevolence of the empowering Spirit, and a sense of engagement with the creativity of the Spirit, beget a whole different understanding of God and humans. We seem to be moving in a collaborative endeavor strongly resonant of John 15:15, "No longer do I call you servants but friends."

Multiple Religious Belonging

Monotheism continues to dominate the contemporary religious landscape. This is a cultural rather than merely a religious phenomenon. Huge swathes of our contemporary culture are addicted to imperial power. Consciously or otherwise this evokes and supports the notion of one powerful deity.

Across many of the major world religions, we observe a new strain of fundamentalism, rooted in an exclusive patriarchal ruling God who will tolerate no other. As indicated previously, a great deal of projection goes on here. We create a God in the image of our own insatiable hunger for domination and control. Then, in our addictive delusion, we worship the monster we have created—and try to force everybody else to do the same. Irrational fear seems to play a large role in this convoluted religiosity.

Fortunately, evolution is empowering us to redress the balance. In this case it is not the survival of the fittest but the co-evolution of those who trust the evolutionary process.

Monotheism continues to dominate the contemporary religious landscape. However, evolution is empowering us to redress the balance in a development known as multiple religious belonging. We can glean its meaning (and its truth) from the following personal description:

> When people ask what I am religiously, I say, "My bowel is Shamanist. My heart is Buddhist. My right brain, which defines my mood, is Confucian and Taoist. My left brain,

> which defines my public language, is Protestant Christian, and overall, my aura is eco-feminist.".... As a Korean woman, I was raised in the 5,000-year-old Shamanist tradition and the 2,000-year-old Taoist-Confucian tradition, with 2,000 years of Buddhist tradition, 100 years of Protestant tradition, and twenty years of eco-feminist tradition. So, my body is like a religious pantheon. I am living with communities of Gods, a continuum of divinity, and a family of religions."[37]

In this evolutionary development, we evidence another type of dying and rising to new life, not merely discarding the particularity of a former belief, but a luring of the Spirit into a newly expanded horizon of meaning.

Re-visioning the Paschal Journey

When Christians reference the paschal journey, it is nearly always in the context of the death and resurrection of Jesus. For much of Christendom, the resurrection of Jesus was viewed in heroic, miraculous terms. Jesus, the perfect representative of the monotheistic powerful God, conquered even death itself, thus reclaiming and reestablishing his divine kingship both here and in the life to come.

Beginning in the mid-twentieth century, some scripture scholars have viewed the resurrection of Jesus in a different light, one that moves us beyond the demonization of death itself but also surfacing another Christological motif, the liberating and empowering Jesus arising within the communal body of believers. This interpretation makes a great deal more sense to adult faith believers in the twenty-first century.

Adopting a more humble, discerning stance, the argument goes like this. Nobody can state for certain what happened to Jesus after his death. Our patriarchal will-to-power finds it hard to accept a largely unanswered reality, a classical dark night of soul and senses. We cannot tolerate a vacuum, despite all that modern science reassures us about the creative dynamic of nature's own vacuum. Moreover, the patriarchal mind-set feels the need to offer a coherent rational answer to all aspects of life, including those that clearly stretch the human imagination and our spiritual intuition.

Why not divert attention to the first witnesses? What was it in that final transformative experience of Jesus that awoke in them an indisputable conviction that Jesus was alive after his earthly death, in fact, more so now than during his earthly life? And was it in the power of that creative arising that they too became the bold witness to all that Jesus lived and died for? In this discerning strategy it is the questions rather than the answers that guide us to deeper truth.

All of which leads us into a massive conundrum! It has been long assumed that it was the twelve apostles who were the primary witnesses to the resurrection of Jesus and thus the ones who laid the foundation of what today we call the church. Once again, patriarchal preference gets in the way. Even a cursory glance at the passion narratives illustrate all too clearly that the twelve had huge problems particularly with the death of Jesus. Allegedly, Judas could not handle it at all, and Peter sounds like somebody facing a nervous breakdown. And where were all the rest? They had fled lest they too might be crucified.

So who remained? Mary Magdalene and a group of followers consisting predominantly of women but very likely inclusive of men as well. According to Luke 23:55, they saw where the body was laid. They are the ones who remain to the very end. They go right into the death experience and do not run away. And in all four Gospels we witness their presence on Easter Sunday morn. The first person to be formally commissioned by the Risen Jesus is Mary Magdalene.[38]

Personally, I don't regard these insights as controversial anymore. The role of women in early Christian times is now well documented and, in the name of justice and truth, must be given the scholarly and religious attention it deserves. Moreover, when we seek to honor the primacy of this alternative apostolic group, and the central role women are playing in it, we enter into those aspects of every paschal journey that Westerners in particular wish to avoid, namely, the *lamenting*, *mourning*, and *grieving*.

This is where the true giftedness of the Gospel women comes to the fore. We are told that the women went away to prepare spices. Unfortunately, the Gospels tell us no more. Even if the anointing with spices did not take place, due to the absence of a body, the anointing is merely one aspect of an elaborate ritual process, marking not merely the death of a loved one but the expression and articulation of the heartbreak and grief involved in losing a loved one. By allowing such grief to come to the fore via lamenting—in other words, by not repressing it—the mourners, particularly the women, were liberated to engage the deeper meaning of all that was happening around them. In a brief, crisp statement, scripture scholar Walter Brueggemann takes us right to the heart of the matter:

> Only grief permits newness.... Where grief is silent, the newness does not come and the old order survives another season. Jesus' main conflict is with the managers of the old order who do not know of its failure and who will do whatever is necessary to keep the grief from becoming visible. For if the grief does not become visible then the charade of the old order can be sustained indefinitely—and newness will never come!... If the hurt is fully expressed and embraced, it liberates God to heal.[39]

The women hold a treacherous, prophetic space, wherein nothing is sure or secure, but everything is open to empowering possibilities that the guardians of orthodoxy can neither imagine nor entertain. This is the same birthing space we encounter in the opening verses of the book of Genesis with the Spirit drawing forth new life from the chaotic depths. It is the paradoxical liberation every mystic knows in the dark night of soul and senses. It is also grounded in the ecstatic birthpangs experienced by every mother giving birth to new life.

At this level of mystical discernment we are invited to embrace the paschal journey at a depth that defies and transcends rational explanation. The Gospel women at Calvary and beyond enter those depths with a quality of courage, insight, and wisdom that Christian believers of our time urgently need. The secret to their integrity and creativity is their ability to ritualize their deep pain and not be overcome by it. Their creative empowerment does not belong merely to the triumph of Pentecost but equally to all those Calvary dark depths of confusion, struggle, and hope.

According to John's Gospel, the "beloved disciple" was with the women on the hill of Calvary.[40] He too underwent the dark night of the soul. We meet him again in John 20:3–8. In this passage loaded with symbolic intrigue, Peter and John are running to the tomb. John, usually interpreted as the believer, gets there first. But there is much more to it than that. After they have reached the tomb, Peter looks in first, and then John. Apparently they both observe the same scene. Yet, when we read the Greek text, two different verbs are employed. For Peter the verb is *theorei*, meaning to contemplate, observe, or scrutinize, but for John it is the verb *eiden*, suggesting perceiving the significance in an intelligent way. Peter employed more sight; John, more insight.

It strikes me that most commentators miss the nuanced mystical meaning here. John is the one who has endured the dark night, walking through the valley of death. He is the first to perceive deeply, whereas Peter, who apparently was not at Calvary, is unable to engage the mystical paradox.

Beyond the Monotheistic Death and Resurrection

Christianity has proudly—indeed arrogantly—proclaimed its version of truth on the basis of the one and only One, who truly was of God and proved it by his readiness to undergo death for the salvation of all and rise again triumphantly to the glory of heaven. Only the Christian Jesus has uniquely accomplished this transformation. He is the only one who truly represents God's will for all humans—and for all creation.

Just as Islam feels unique for many Muslims, and Hinduism for several Hindus, so does Christianity for the Christian people. For many Christians that means clinging exclusively to the Christian way. To do otherwise feels like betrayal for many Christians. Even within the Christian denominations themselves, people retain quite a distance; for fundamentalist Christians, participation in one another's religious services, even entering another church building, is deemed inappropriate, disrespectful, and, for some, a deviation.

Our monotheistic legacy has left us with several false impressions. Not even in its foundational context do we find a uniform outline of the Christian faith. Not merely was early Christianity deeply wedded to Judaism. It was also intimately entwined with the several pagan religions that proliferated at the time. The basic texts on which the veracity of the faith is based—the four Gospels—were edited extensively right up until the end of the fourth century. Early Christianity had to deal with far more disunity than unity. Pluriformity, and not conformity, was the order of the day.

Our monotheistic exclusivity is not about Jesus or Gospel-based faith. It is the legacy of our imperial collusion with patriarchal power, a historical deviation that has long outlived its usefulness. It is a faith system that contravenes all that is sacred and liberating in terms of a paschal journey. We cling to idols that we need to let die, and when we do allow them to die we open ourselves to the Spirit's ever-new empowerment rising up in that graced awakening we call resurrection.

Mary Magdalene and her associates, deeply versed in the art of grieving, knew how to die to the old and open themselves to the liberating power of the new. They provide the prophetic inspiration for their time and for ours. We have too long ignored them, and bizarrely have tried to suppress their primordial witness.

In every articulation of resurrection to new life, we evidence a stretching of horizons taking us far beyond the old, but frequently without clear alternative strategies. Often, it is more a case of the road being made by walking. And the authenticity of this endeavor largely depends on who I am making the journey with. Truth tends to arise from the dialogue and mutual exploration of kindred spirits. It is a truth from the ground up rather than from the top down.

Critics are quick to denounce this evolutionary thrust, in terms of its perceived individualism and narcissistic self-preoccupation, frequently overlooking the social dimension and the extensive employment of friendship-based networking today.

To suggest that monotheism is dying—or even diminishing—sounds preposterous and ridiculous to the millions who have an investment in the preservation and promotion of patriarchal power. For those entrusted with positions of authority, whether in state or church, or in the maintenance of the several institutions upheld by both, the notion of the demise of monotheism is inconceivable; even to entertain such a notion is to open the floodgates for relativism, chaos, and anarchy.

The information explosion of recent decades is awakening a deeper critical consciousness across the human population. More people ask questions and expect informed answers. More people explore various options and tend to distrust those who suggest there is only one authentic version of the truth. Almost unknown to ourselves, millions among us have become more fluid and diverse in our engagement with life. The monolithic mind-set belongs to a former evolutionary stage that is now in irreversible decline.

CHAPTER SIX

Entangled with the Earth

> *Shall we prolong the painful split between mind and body by continuing to neglect our carnal entanglement with this immense Presence, or shall we finally heal the age-old wound by acknowledging earth's implicit involvement in all our experience—as the solid ground that supports all our certainties, and the distant horizon that provides all our dreams.*
>
> —David Abram

As a child I was often reminded of my Celtic origins, a distinctive allegiance that supposedly made me better than many others and specifically superior to the archenemy of my people, namely, the Brits. Amid such acculturation, the embedded wisdom of my Celtic roots was both neglected and suppressed. Fortunately, I can recall a range of experiences assuring me that the Celtic spirit is deeply insinuated in my being and knows how to nourish me despite the setbacks of life's journey.

My inner acquaintance with the bioregion of my birth bestows a visceral knowledge, an ecological intimacy, that endures across many thresholds. Intuitively I know the call of the early dawn and the balm of a crimson sunset. I relish the wind's energy blowing in my face as I roam beloved mountains or lie still on the grass of the meadows I cherished as a child. I feel an affinity with the stately oak trees, while the emergence of the first snowdrops evokes my tender care. As I hold a handful of uncontaminated soil, I realize I am gazing into the depths of my own soul.

Now that I have outgrown the dualistic splitting of my inherited faith formation—the binary distinctions between sacred and secular, body and soul, matter and spirit—I can revisit and reclaim the deeper truths that nature awakened in my soul. How to integrate this wisdom continues to be a formidable challenge, particularly in an Ireland so attached to corporate values and capitalist economics. Everything has become a commodity for human use and for peddling the profits of trade. But residual wisdom endures, and in the face of the imminent ecological crisis of the twenty-first century, I hope it can be retrieved to the benefit of my own people and that of the wider human family.

The Tree of Life

Like every Celt, I love trees. They fascinate and intrigue me. Trees draw me to an ancient spiritual wisdom long known to the human species. The tree was a primary symbol of the Great Earth Mother Goddess worshiped by our ancestors some forty thousand years ago. The book of Genesis knows that ancient wisdom, though some of the people who wrote or edited the book may not have shared that knowledge. Because of their misogynist fear of the feminine they screwed up the ancient relationship between the woman and the tree. As a result both end up deeply wounded.

When the tree calls, I can hear primal echoes, which, I guess, is what happened in the spring of 1975 when I ended up at a Lenten talk in Coventry Cathedral in the United Kingdom. The speaker was a botanist who spoke of the spirituality of trees. In fact, it was the botany, and not merely the spirituality, that fascinated me.

Beginning with the colloquial wisdom, whereby trees draw their nourishment primarily, if not exclusively, from their roots, he informed us that this was a popular understanding that no longer made any scientific sense. It described the tree as a closed system, containing within itself all it needed to grow and flourish, when in truth a tree is an open system. As an open system the tree flourishes through an intricate interrelationship with several organic forces within a scientific process known as photosynthesis (how the energy of sunlight becomes a nourishing source for all organic life).

While trees come in several shapes, the botanist informed us that evolution had selected two configurations most commonly seen throughout the arboreal world. One is the cone shape and the other the canopy (like an open umbrella). These seem to be the shapes best suited for the tree to absorb the energy of sunlight, a major contributory factor to the growth and development of the tree.

Sunlight contributes at least 50 percent of the growth energy for the tree. Rainwater and moisture contribute at least another 20 percent, air a further 10 percent, and various other ingredients involved in photosynthesis add another 10 percent. All of which brings us to 90 percent—and all coming from outside the tree, not from within it.[41] It is important to note here that the inner and outer cannot be kept apart. That dualistic distinction makes no sense when we view the tree as a holistic process of becoming. The inner and the outer are one.

As a child and a young adult I was heavily indoctrinated on the importance of roots, particularly those of my Irish identity and my Catholic faith. Those were my solid roots that required lifelong devotion, challenging me to keep deepening those roots, with the unambiguous message that the deeper I sank those roots the more authentic I would be. How could my wisdom-bearers have been so blind? Look at a tree toppled over in a storm, and it is crystal clear: the roots of a tree spread out; they don't grow deep! (Except in very dry sandy conditions.)

Roots are essential to the existence of a tree and always will be. Moreover, human tampering with the roots can easily destroy and kill a tree. When it comes to the growth of a tree, however, the roots contribute very little. Since a tree is an open system, its flourishing arises from its *interdependence*, not from its *rootedness.*

Preoccupation with rootedness, of the type so prevalent in my early formative years, arises from a false understanding of human culture and God's creation. Nothing in creation flourishes primarily via rootedness; nothing makes sense on its own. All is interconnected; everything flourishes through interdependence. The preoccupation with rootedness arises from a sense of psychic insecurity, itself based on a superficial understanding on how creation functions—at every level. The tree is indeed a potent, ageless symbol of how creation thrives, of how the divine life force co-creates with our unfolding creation. Humans need to adjust to this divine, cosmic imperative. Otherwise, we are condemning ourselves to anomie and alienation, out of step with the foundational meaning of all existence.

From the Personal to the Transpersonal

Informed by this deeper wisdom symbolized in the tree, the transformative process (resurrection) becomes significantly clearer. Instead of clinging to my Irish roots, over against every other nationalistic force, I am invited to embrace the transnational identity of becoming more deeply European, more expansively planetary, and more deeply cosmic. Paradoxically, it is in transcending my exclusive Irish identity that I grow more deeply into it.

And similarly with my Catholic faith, the invitation is to become more of an ecumenical Christian, open to multifaith dialogue and engagement and, eventually, embracing the universal spiritual empowerment of the God who works throughout the entire creation. This is not an abandonment of my Catholicism; rather, it is a more authentic espousal of catholicity in its deeper meaning.

Entanglement is how quantum physics names this pervasive interdependence. Nothing makes sense in isolation, nor must the interdependent context be confined merely to human beings. Our convivial relationship with creation—at both cosmic and planetary levels—is foundational to all we are and all we are invited to become. It transcends all the roots that ground us, inviting us to enlarged horizons that forever engage our spirit and imagination.

Quantum Entanglement

The tree is an icon of God at work in creation. In Christian theology we describe it as the Trinitarian God, the subject of much theological controversy throughout the ages. Beyond the metaphysical rhetoric lies a deeper layer like that of the root system in the redwood forests. All is interconnected. Entanglement is how it is named in quantum physics, a concept that will need to be integrated into a transpersonal theology for our future.

The evolutionary imperative of our time could be described as operating on overdrive, compensating, as it were, for the false and debilitating identity out of which we have been operating for the past few millennia. The very suggestion that we have been doing things in a wrong way for a few thousand years is likely to sound weird and preposterous to many. We have been so conditioned to a reductionistic view of reality, locked into closed systemic thinking.

None of our systems—educational, political, economic, or religious—has been telling us the truth, and in our inherited gullibility, we have been colluding with their very narrow view of reality. Our true human story of *seven million years* has been neither recognized nor affirmed. For much of that time we lived in a more entangled way, congruent with our place in a quantum universe. We lived very close to nature, engaging in a convivial manner with its organic nurturance, enhancing its growth and development, with the earth in turn supporting our human endeavor.

It would seem we got it right most of the time, till about ten thousand years ago when the so-called agricultural revolution disrupted and undermined the creative balance. A whole range of new diseases appeared for the first time. We began treating the earth as a commodity to be usurped and subdued. We lost sense of our entanglement, our interdependence with the cosmic and planetary web of life.

It is that dislocation, and its consequent deleterious impact, that is at the root of many of the major problems facing humanity today. We are a species who have lost our way. Many of the major crises of this time, however, particularly those of an ecological and environmental nature, are alerting us to our impending demise and calling us to new ways of being in our world. That is the evolutionary imperative I allude to throughout this book.

It is as if evolution is trying to save us from ourselves, from our addiction to patriarchal power, and from our insatiable desire to conquer all before us. We are losing that battle and are in danger of ourselves becoming its biggest losers. We need to become entangled once more and reclaim a more benign and convivial relationship with the wider web of creation.

Creation Spirituality

Our emerging sense of spirituality is moving us in the right direction, despite the reactionary opposition from formal religionists. The integration of faith with the pressing contemporary ecological issues is central to the transpersonal shift I describe throughout this book. For myself that shift began around 1985 when a good friend gifted me with a copy of Matthew Fox's book *Original Blessing*. That was my first introduction to creation spirituality, in an ever-deepening process of retrieving my Celtic earth-wisdom but, more important, exploring its significance for our precarious earthly situation. Initially, *Original Blessing* served the deeper integration in my own spiritual emergence, healing the dualistic splitting (referred to above) while also introducing me to the great mystical traditions of our Christian story.

Names such as Meister Eckhart, Hildegard of Bingen, Mechthild of Magdeburg, Julian of Norwich were almost entirely new to me, as was the notion that *mysticism* is not so much about some kind of elevated suspension out of this world, but rather an intimate relationship with God in and through the intimacy of creation, which is exactly what the scientific notion of entanglement denotes.[42] The body is the medium through which we all connect with our earthiness. Born of the earth, our bodies know their deep affinity with soil and the possibility of being at home in the earth. Even at the personal level, many of us are not grounded in our bodies. At the transpersonal level, the needed integration is even more challenging. As a starting point, we need to come to terms with the fact that God loves bodies and loves all bodies unconditionally. It is in and through bodies that the creative energy of the Spirit flows. Without body Spirit can achieve nothing.

God's primary body manifesting to us, and bestowing on us, God's own life is that of the evolving universe itself, the operational sphere in which the creativity of the Holy One has been at work for billions of years before humans, religions, or churches ever came to be. It is in the universe at large that we discern the empowering creativity of God, elegant while being simultaneously highly paradoxical (as I explain in chapter four). *The universe is God's primary revelation for us and to us.* Therein the face of the Holy One is first made real for humans.

Embodiment

Accordingly, nothing in creation can be adequately explained in material, physical, or biological terms. The divine radiance is in the interconnectedness of all the apparently separate elements. The embodiment in question is not about product but about process. It is in the co-evolutionary unfolding of reality that we encounter the elegance and magnificence of the divine creativity.[43]

Our human experience of this cosmic sense of embodiment is mediated for us in and through our earthiness, which in turn is facilitated through all the earth-creatures with which we share our convivial existence. Here we encounter a marked departure from all the major religions, which postulate, in one form or another, that our eventual salvation with God is obtained by escaping the curse of this vale of tears. Instead, we are meant to transcend our human predicament so that in death we can escape from our embodiment in creation and be reunited with God in the noncorporeal realm of the afterlife.

In the evolutionary expansive horizons of the twenty-first century, a very different theology calls us forth. It is in the earthly dimensions of our embodiment that we most directly encounter the divine energy that creates and sustains everything in creation. Our earthiness is the umbilical cord that connects us with the birthing and sustaining nature of God. It is at this juncture that we reconnect with indigenous peoples around the world for whom the notion of the Great Spirit provides the primordial identity of the God who energizes everything in our cosmic-planetary being and becoming.

Accordingly, the divine initiative, in terms of incarnation, is not in the historical person of Jesus, nor in the Creator, God the Father, but in that understanding of God we name as Holy Spirit.[44] In our inherited theological understanding of incarnation, there has been one, and only one, foundational meaning: namely, the coming of God into our world in and through the historical person, Jesus of Nazareth.

We need to note clearly the presuppositions being employed:

a) God never really came into the earthly, human realm until the historical moment some two thousand years ago marking the birth, death, and resurrection of Jesus.
b) Jesus came primarily, if not exclusively, for humans, not for the rest of creation.
c) Only Jesus, through the power of his death and resurrection, can rescue sinful humanity from its flawed condition and offer reliable assurance of eternal happiness and salvation.
d) No other religion has anything comparable to the Jesus event; therefore, only Christianity has the fullness of God's revelation.

In the faith passed on to me by my culture and my church, these were unquestioned assumptions. They still remain so for most of my peers and for many preachers and teachers in the Catholic tradition. They are also widely adopted by those Christians who take scripture and church teaching literally. Inherent to this inherited evangelization is a message—often subtle and sometimes overt—that one should not question the truthfulness of the faith or doubt the credulity of those designated to pass it on, particularly catechists and pastors.

Today, millions do doubt; they ask questions and explore alternative ways of living their inherited faith. And for many the very notion of God has changed dramatically. For the purposes of the present work, I find the following challenge from the American theologian John D. Caputo to be particularly relevant: "I do not take the name of God to be the name of a being, of an existent, but of a way I have been overtaken by the world.... We are in this thing together, we and God, and we cannot let each other down. What thing is that? The thing of the world. The thing of it is the world."[45] That reclaiming of holy mystery at the heart of creation is where the Spirit pulsates today. Spirituality is the name of this rediscovery.

Reclaiming the Great Spirit

Spirituality evolves and unfolds around one central idea: *Spirit connecting with spirit.* Everything in creation (not merely humans) is energized from a primordial "entangled" source we call Spirit (with a capital S). The inherited energy in each living organism, and even in the minute subatomic elements that constitute everything in creation, is a manifestation of the same spirit (with a small s). This manifestation of spirit in the human person is what the famous Catholic theologian Karl Rahner had in mind when he described humans as being essentially open to transcendence. Spirit (with a small s) is forever being lured into the dynamic creative energizing of the Great Spirit.

I first encountered the notion of God as Great Spirit in a brief engagement with the Australian aborigines, in 2000 CE, and have had several exposures since then in different parts of the world. This is how indigenous/First Nations people name and understand that divine reality we call God. There is a marked difference, however. For our indigenous peoples, the Great Spirit is not a transcendent reality but an empowering, energizing life force, intimately interwoven (entangled) with the alive Earth itself.[46]

It is in and through our identity and status as Earthlings that we encounter and engage with the Great Spirit. First Nations peoples do not worship the Great Spirit. Their several elaborate rituals are used to sensitize people to the energizing dynamism of the Spirit and to empower them to work collaboratively with the Spirit. And Spirit is not merely in the constructive experiences of life; it also operates in the storms, the sufferings, the setbacks, all that constitutes the great paradox described earlier in this book. Faith in the Great Spirit knows no dualisms.

In all probability, this is the oldest understanding of God known to humans. In former times, we described it as animism, often viewed in derogatory fashion as primitive, tribalistic, and narcissistic. Today, even indigenous peoples themselves are losing sight of the profound depth of this ancient belief system.

Submerged within all the major religions of our time are traces of our ancient faith in God as the Great Spirit. The wisdom arising from both quantum physics and the new cosmology provides an aperture into this foundational, transpersonal faith. Conventional theology being too narrowly anthropocentric has not even woken up yet to this empowering belief system. When we do, some major adjustments will ensue from several of our prevailing doctrines.

None are more urgent than the foundations of our Judeo-Christian story. When we read the opening chapters of the book of Genesis in a more discerning way, it is difficult to overlook the fact that it is the Spirit who comes first, energizing all possibility from the primordial depths, *ex profundis* rather than *ex nihilo*. Genesis 1:1 opens with the Spirit, not with the Father-creator, drawing forth creative energy from the depths. The creator's ability to beget—conventionally named as God the Father—is itself empowered by the Great Spirit.[47] And it is in the power of that same Spirit that Jesus is called into mission (Mark 1:9–11) and raised from the dead (Romans 1:4; 8:11).

In the contemporary transpersonal realm, spirituality is outpacing theology. By honoring the primary role of the energizing Spirit, spirituality begins to highlight and unravel the complex and creative web of life in which everything is deeply interconnected. All this is the work of the Spirit in what contemporary science describes as a flat universe, that is, a world without beginning or end. The Spirit *is* and always will be.[48]

Reframing the Story of Pentecost

According to the conventional Christian narrative, God sent the embodied Jesus to rescue humanity from its inherited deprivation of original sin. The rescue, however, was largely done in a disembodied way, with a confused patriarchal mind-set that seriously undermines everything the Great Spirit represents. According to the infancy narratives of Matthew and Luke, Jesus came into the world not through the God-given process of human birthing, that is, via embodied sexual intercourse, but by a divine miraculous implanting of Jesus in Mary's womb.[49]

At the other end of his earthly life, he is elevated out of the world, in order to mediate liberation for sinful humans. He has to sacrifice all that is unique to his embodied condition in order to rescue humanity. One gets a sense that his earthly body is a barrier that has to be removed, so that his pure spirit can achieve God's desires. And in the resurrection, although we are dealing with some kind of reconstituted body, it obviously is not an earthly one but some type of divine organism that enters the human realm yet remains transcendent to it.

Of course, the biggest problem with our conventional death-resurrection narrative is the substantial displacement of the earthly life of Jesus. It feels as if the life of Jesus, and its hugely transformative significance as a Spirit-filled inheritance, is merely a preparation for the real stuff that came in the last few days of his earthly existence. Salvation and redemption do not belong to the exemplary life of Jesus but to his death and resurrection.

By the end of the Gospel narratives, the Great Spirit has been reduced to the Holy Spirit whose energizing can be done only after Father and Son have accomplished the anthropocentric deliverance. What is still considered to be an event of enormous importance—indeed the very foundation of the church itself—is now in need of radical reformulation. I refer to the Pentecost event described in Acts 2:1–11 in these words:

> When Pentecost day came round, all the believers were gathered in one room when suddenly they heard what sounded like a powerful wind from Heaven, the noise of which filled the entire house where they were sitting; and something appeared to them that seemed like tongues of fire; these separated and came to rest on the head of each of them. They were all filled with the Holy Spirit and began to speak foreign languages, as the Spirit gave them the gift of speech. Now there were dwelling in Jerusalem Jews, devout people from every nation under heaven. And at this sound the multitude came together, and they were bewildered, because each one heard them speaking in his own native language. "Are not all these who are speaking Galileans?" they asked. "How is it that we each hear them in our own native languages? Parthians, Medes and Elamites…people form Judea and Cappadocia, Egypt and parts of Libya…. Visitors from Rome, both Jews and proselytes. We hear them telling in our own tongues the mighty works of God."

This text is used each year by all Christian denominations for the liturgies of Pentecost Sunday. There are two parts to this passage. The first is that of 2:1–4, which describes the scene in the Upper Room (cf. Acts 1:12ff.) where the twelve are gathered.[50] According to earliest Christian belief, articulated particularly through art and legend, the gathered group experienced a kind of mystical transformation in which fiery tongues of flame descended on each one of them, empowering them with the gift of speech, understood as a divine mandate to go forth to preach and teach the message of the Gospel.

Then there is the second section: Acts 2:5–11, describing a diverse group of ordinary people, from lands that have not yet been evangelized, and these appropriate the impact of what is going on with an unexpected sense of spiritual receptivity. Although the spirit-filled preachers are using one language, those listening can hear them, each in their own language, and can comprehend the spiritual import as a message that evokes the praise and glory of God. The capacity for this kind of receptivity is generally considered to be an achievement commonly known as *the grace of discernment*, involving deep listening, wise comprehension, and informed spiritual response. According to those versed in the skills of Christian discernment, this is a gifted grace that presumes a deep faith in the living Spirit of God.

Nowhere in the opening chapters of Acts are we told that this second group (in Acts 2:5–11) has been conferred with the gift of the Spirit. According to Acts 2:1–4, that gift has been given only to the twelve preachers. It is from and through the twelve that every other Christian will learn to preach and teach the Gospel. So, how do we make sense of what is going on in this perplexing text? And why is it that in the typical preaching of Pentecost Sunday—all over the Christian world—much attention is given to the first passage (2:1–4) with scant attention, if any at all, to the second section, Acts 2:5–11?

What is Luke's understanding of the Holy Spirit? According to Acts 2:1–4, the Spirit is a divine life force, some kind of mystical organism, capable of reinvigorating select human beings (all male) so that they become more effective in preaching and teaching the Gospel of Jesus. The Spirit seems to be supporting and affirming the patriarchal bias that dominated the evolution of the early church. This might be regarded as an exclusive view, significantly different from the second part of chapter two (5–11) where inclusiveness comes to the fore.

We have no way of ascertaining how Luke understood the second section of the Pentecost reading, other than highlighting these diverse visitors as being at one in their admiration for the twelve preachers. But there is a great deal more than admiration going on in this scenario. As indicated above, these diverse peoples, allegedly not yet evangelized, seem to be endowed with some remarkable gifts for discernment, gifts that all the great religions deem to be uniquely of God's own spirit.

A more responsible Christian interpretation requires us to consider that this amorphous, "unevangelized" group of Acts 2:5–11 is already filled with the Holy Spirit. Why? Because as indicated by Genesis 1:1, the whole creation is replete with the empowering creativity of the Holy Spirit. Every creature in that same creation, human and nonhuman alike, is already blessed with the fullness of God's Spirit. The primacy of the Spirit, therefore, belongs to the second group rather than to the first. The true witness to Holy Spirit is with the second rather than with the first group.

Luke's theology of the Holy Spirit fits well with the popular church's teaching of a descending patriarchal Trinity, attributing a vague and ill-defined role to the third "person." Luke lacks all sense of the exuberance of the indigenous notion of the *Great Spirit.* In this atrophied anthropocentric account, we have lost the transpersonal ambit that embraces all creation and the more generic understanding of the embracing mystery, the Spirit of God inhabiting, energizing, and empowering the whole creation.

An Entangled Paschal Journey

The bioregional grounding I experienced as a child has in a sense come full circle and spirals into some of the enlarged entangled horizons explored in the present chapter. I can now see how so much of my early formative influence was undermined by the devotional religiosity that characterized the culture of the time. All the emphasis lay on fidelity to the church and the fulfillment of religious obligation to guarantee the salvation of one's individual soul. Human personhood itself was disenfranchised. Only the soul mattered within a very narrow, individualistic sense of personhood.

It was also a culture in which dualistic splitting was extremely accentuated. There was no meeting ground between sacred and secular. God belonged to the heavenly abode well above this sinful vale of tears where for some inexplicable reason humans had to endure a journey of travail. In the words of Brigitte Kahl, "Binaries are omnivores and ravenous. Once in place they devour everything in their reach—fowl and fish, men and mice—metabolizing them into one big polarity of us versus them."[51]

Dualistic religiosity dominated the landscape—and much of the surrounding culture. Yet, to gain the benefits of such religiosity one had to go to church on Sundays and adhere to the will of God as the clergy dictated. Long before the issue of clerical sex abuse came to the fore, the prevailing religiosity had abuse deeply inscribed at its core.

I was one of the fortunate ones, blessed with the breakthrough my religious life made possible for me. I have encountered people disillusioned, angry, and hurt because of this early dysfunctional faith formation. Far more prevalent, however, are those whose stories—unfortunately—have not been recorded or for various reasons never got the attention they deserved. These include the narratives of so many indigenous peoples scattered all over our world today. In many cases, these are disciples of the Great Spirit, still awaiting their hour of liberation.

Such people have their forerunners, the amorphous group described in Acts 2:5–11. Those ignored voices in Acts 2:5–11, along with the subdued voices of many contemporary peoples, need to be both heard anew and incorporated into the discerning spiritual landscape of the twenty-first century. Hopefully, the insights of science and cosmology, the urgent ecological forces of our age, the deepening insights into scripture and theology, and the wisdom garnered by the growing body of adult faith seekers, all contribute to a more inclusive and empowering spiritual culture for now and for the decades ahead.

In that "entangled" journey there is a great deal of death and rising to new life. At one level there is nothing entirely new in what I am proposing. The Great Spirit has been ploughing these fertile furrows ever since the dawn of time. The birthing creative life force has begotten life-forms in abundance. The tree of life has flourished and borne much fruit. On that grand scale, resurrection has outwitted Calvary many times over. Hope prevails!

For too long we have been clinging to an old metaphysical God-concept, preoccupied with defending its own unilateral power. That paradigm is effectively dead, although political, economic, and ecclesiastical power clings on desperately. And many deluded humans go along with a postcolonial residue that has outlived its usefulness. As we move deeper into the twenty-first century, the paradigm will either progressively fall apart (which is already happening) or may quite suddenly implode on itself (likely to happen to Islam before other major religions). This old paradigm is just too alien to the evolutionary thrust of cosmic and earthly life today for it to survive.

Its demise will engage us in a major paschal journey, but that energizing Spirit will blow where she wills and as she wills. At the end of the day, she will bring about a resurrection breakthrough, every bit as earth-shattering and empowering as any of the Christian renderings we have known over the past two thousand years. Except, this time round, the Earth itself will play a more central role transcending the anthropocentric arrogance of the past. Either that, or humanity itself will undergo a mass crucifixion.

CHAPTER SEVEN

The Death and Resurrection of Liberation

> *The presence of the wide, evolving cosmos calls for a genuinely new paradigm, different from the anthropocentric concern with human sin in the context of feudal obligations. We need to turn the page on satisfaction theory and allow it to take a well-deserved rest.*
>
> —Elizabeth Johnson.

I first encountered the real pain of human mortality in the tragic death of my niece, Pauline. Just a few years later I was to encounter death in a more graphic and frightening way. It happened in 2003, in the city of Lusaka, capital of Zambia in East Africa.

Although I had been given the outline of the horrific story, nothing could have prepared me for the encounter with Martha, with a forlorn face etched with a depth of grief that defied all sense and meaning.

Martha's husband had died in a road accident many years previously, leaving her with eight children, all of whom married and among them parented thirty-two children, of which Martha was the proud grandmother. Tragedy began to strike in the early 1990s, as AIDS/HIV consumed all before it amid several groups across the African continent. Between 1991 and 2002, in a space of eleven years, Martha buried all her eight offspring, all their spouses, and two of her grandchildren.

When I was introduced to Martha by a religious sister, one of her support team, I recall a distinctive sense of paralysis consisting of numbness and unspeakable rage. The numbness was my defense against the appalling grief and hopelessness of the entire situation. My rage, as I shall indicate below, had to do with the injustice whereby Martha and the African peoples could not get access to the retroviral drugs that were altering the very nature of AIDS/HIV in the rich West.

The Devotion of Consolation

In the desperation of the moment, all I can recall saying to Martha was: "How in the name of God do you cope and survive?" She pointed up to a large crucifix in the hall where we met and said: "Thank God he died for me, because if he had not died for me, I would not be able to continue." The sister accompanying her intervened and added: "Martha has a wonderful devotion to the crucified Jesus. She begins and ends each day kissing her crucifix. It gives her comfort, consolation, and strength." And the sister continued: "And despite her great struggle trying to support and care for the remaining thirty grandchildren, Martha prays every day, specifically eighteen decades of the Rosary, one decade for each of her deceased children, a decade for each of their spouses, and two decades for the deceased grandchildren. And she makes many novenas, the one to the Sacred Heart being her favorite."

On top of all my other confused feelings, I was keenly aware of my sense of guilt. Clearly everybody was admiring Martha for her faith-based resilience, but not me! The raging sense of injustice in my heart left me totally bewildered.

From 1989 until 1995, I myself had worked as an AIDS/HIV counselor in London. My ministry began under the dark cloud of an impending pandemic, what many were describing as an imminent plague. In those days when we visited affected people in hospitals (and in their homes) we had to don protective plastic clothing from head to foot. Even though there was no evidence for direct transmission, nobody was entirely sure.

As we entered the 1990s, the miracle retroviral drug known as AZT came on stream, and within a few months we began to notice improvements, encouraged by the news coming out of the United States of people now living fairly normal lives, despite the fact that they had full-blown AIDS. I witnessed the same optimistic scene in the United Kingdom before moving on to another ministry in 1995.

Meanwhile, we were hearing of the horror stories coming out of Africa. Whole families, and even some tribes, were being decimated by the illness. While millions of Westerners were living well with the disease, millions of Africans were capitulating to its onslaught. We all knew why. Pharmaceutical companies were not prepared to share the resources with those who could not pay the money. Financial profit rather than saving human lives was the blunt and harsh truth.

And Martha continued praying. So did millions of others. But the prayers and devotions were neither halting the deadly onslaught nor converting the hardened hearts of Western profiteers. Of course, the prayers and devotions kept people going, reassuring them of some semblance of meaning and hope in a truly hopeless situation.

The Spirituality of Liberation

Whether by the sheer weight of the hunger for justice, or the desperate reaction of people who knew that only a drastic solution would work, a breakthrough happened in 2003. The details are sketchy and are unlikely ever to come to public knowledge. It seems that a small group of activists—presumably with some scientific and medical expertise—managed to reproduce the copyright for some of the prevailing retroviral drugs and began manufacturing them secretly, initially in India it seems, and from there they were able to transport them readily and cheaply into East Africa. Shortly thereafter the manufacturing itself moved to Africa.

Now, the deprived people of Africa could get access to the drugs and, quite similar to the West, a decline in the death rate was noted in a matter of months. Fortunately for Martha, she and her family were among the first to receive the drugs, and without them she would have had more deaths and untimely funerals among her remaining thirty grandchildren.

She was now the beneficiary of empowering hope, something the devotions and multiple prayers could never have achieved. Since we know nothing of those brave risk-takers, we can only guess what motivated them to do what they did. I have no hesitation in calling them *prophetic* with the full spiritual and theological weight of that word. For me they are pioneers of what I now describe as the spirituality of liberation. They themselves might have little or no religious faith. That does not matter. What they delivered is among the most credible and compelling evidence I have ever known of what the Gospels call the kingdom of God.

From the Personal to the Transpersonal

Personal devotion features in every major world religion. It creates and maintains a sense of intimacy between the devotee and God (variously understood). It helps to bring God near and reassures the devotee that God does care and love. Devotion is a major feature of what is often described as a personal relationship with God (or with Jesus). I name it the devotion of consolation.

There is a shadow side to devotional faith, rarely acknowledged by formal churches, since they themselves find devotions an effective way to exercise domination and control over believers. Devotions thrive on a codependent relationship in which a childlike, unworthy (and often fearful) devotee beseeches an all-powerful deity for help and assistance. The posture is sometimes described as throwing oneself at the mercy of God.

The spirituality of liberation is of a very different persuasion. Its foundational premise is that we are all loved unconditionally by God, so we don't need to beseech or persuade God for anything. What we need to be about is making real for others the empowering love with which we ourselves are unconditionally loved. Here everybody is seen as an adult and not as a passive child. The mediation of love, therefore, can never be patronizing toward, or merely appeasing for, the vulnerable other. Instead, it must empower and liberate others to become agents for their own growth and development.

The Desired Integration

Despite the negative appraisal of religion in the modern world, millions still rely on a devotional faith to help them through lives of struggle, pain, and suffering. We can easily dismiss such devotionalism by citing Karl Marx's claim that religion is the opium of the people,[52] but often such practices are subtly woven into survival strategies without which despair would engulf many lives, condemned to oppression, poverty, and the appalling conditions no human should have to endure.

More significantly, we are dealing with a religious dynamic that is deep and complex, supporting some of the most sophisticated mystical movements ever known to humans. Here we touch into the transpersonal, experienced in mystics and sages as wonder, amazement, joy, ecstasy, delight. These are not mere fleeting sensations but emotions that evoke the awesomeness of mystery, enriching our lives with deeper meaning.

If we get rid of devotions, as allegedly mainline Protestantism tried to do in the sixteenth and seventeenth centuries, we rob our faith of the very elements that constitute its deeper meaning, the ingredients that ground for us the empowering presence of the Godhead itself. The challenge facing us is one of integration. How do we reclaim devotional elements so that they empower us to embrace the daring, liberating, and empowering capacities that authenticate genuine religion?

For Christianity as for all authentic religion, transformation is the primary goal, empowering us to create on earth a set of values that draw forth all that is good and wholesome in humans and in all aspects of the web of life. Authentic spirituality seeks to empower our human endeavor to create a better world for all beings. The spirituality of liberation is our primary task, not merely a freedom from, but, more important, a freedom for. The millions trapped in poverty, violence, and oppression certainly deserve to be freed from all that immobilizes and weighs them down, while those living in the lap of luxury, or ruthlessly exploiting the earth for mere human gain, also need to be set free—to live in a more convivial and responsible way within the web of universal life.

The Long Road to Freedom

Ever since humans became ensnared in the commodification of the land, some ten thousand years ago, there has been a progressive deterioration in our health and well-being and a growing sense of alienation in relation to our status as Earthlings. To resolve the organic disconnection that we ourselves created, we invented a Sky-God to rescue us from our own stupidity. Our relationship with this powerful divine king (above the sky) became ever more dysfunctional as we sought to placate the deity with a range of sacrificial rituals. The slaughtering and offering up of the sacrificial lamb became one of the best known to both Jews and Christians.

The Christian emphasis on *atonement*—describing Jesus as the Lamb of God who takes away the sins of the world—seems to be rooted in the feast of Yom Kippur in the Hebrew Scriptures (described in the book of Leviticus, chapters 16 and 23). John Shelby Spong persuasively argues that it is our gentile-inherited tendency to literalize events like Yom Kippur—frequently distorting the original Jewish context—that leaves us with a grossly convoluted understanding of atonement, in both the Old Testament setting and in its application to the death of Jesus. One particular aspect of the atonement theory requiring a more discerning scrutiny is that of sacrifice. The sacrifice of lambs played a central role in the faith of the Jews.[53]

In the Passover feast, one of the main Jewish holidays marking God's deliverance of the Israelites from bondage in Egypt, the slaying of the Passover lamb and the consequent application of the blood to doorposts of the houses (Exodus 12:11–13) evoked the deliverance into new freedom and for the Jewish people a reintegration into their own land. Sacrificing lambs in the temple was a daily occurrence, a ritual to mark the forgiveness of sins. Both Jeremiah and Isaiah foretold the coming of One who would be brought "like a lamb led to the slaughter" (Jeremiah 11:19; Isaiah 53:7) and whose sufferings and sacrifice would provide redemption for Israel.

Understandably, then, the early Jewish-Christians would view the death of Jesus against this background, and we have long assumed that Jesus himself would have done the same. But this assumption loses credibility, at least on two fronts:

a) The celebration of Yom Kippur (and the accompanying ritual of sacrifice) was a symbol of human yearning for perfection, and not about victimization to placate an angry God.[54]
b) Second, if we take seriously the Gospel strategy of the new empowering companionship (the kingdom), we cannot avoid the inescapable truth that salvation and redemption (if we wish to retain such language) come through the *life* of Jesus

> and not merely through his death. In fact, it is much more congruent to understand his death as the price paid for a life radically lived.

In this context, sacrifice indeed holds a central place. Its primary meaning from the original Latin is to *make something sacred*, and not merely to give something up as conventionally understood. The giving-up aspect is still significant, however, describing a sacrificial element visible throughout the entire creation. For example, every day the sun sacrifices tons of energy to make possible the process of photosynthesis through which the entire food chain is energized. Many species have to endure sacrifice, and some do so altruistically, for the sake of others. In this sense sacrifice is a key element of empowering love and a central feature of the paschal dynamic at work throughout the whole creation.

It is the sacrifices that Jesus made in his lifetime—to bring about empowering and liberating justice for people and creation alike—that require our discerning attention, not what happened merely in his death experience. Jesus was killed because he was so empowering for the disillusioned, alienated people that the political and ecclesiastical systems of the day could tolerate him no longer and felt they had to get rid of him. Jesus took on the full weight of the paschal journey, and for Christians to this day he remains an inspiring and empowering example of one whose death and resurrection was not merely about human salvation, but about a new empowering liberation for all life, human and nonhuman alike. In the words of theologian Elizabeth Johnson, "Calvary graphically shows that the God of suffering love abides in solidarity with all creatures, bearing the cost of new life through endless millennia of evolution, from the extinction of whole species to, yes, every sparrow that falls to the ground."[55]

The Disempowering Cross

In Martha's story, at the beginning of this chapter, we see a Christian for whom the crucifix, the image of the crucified Jesus, is not merely an icon of central importance; effectively, it is the heart and soul of her faith in God. And for myself, right into my early adult years, it also symbolized the primary meaning of my faith. It was in and through the power of the cross that I, and all sinful people, would be saved. And without that exemplary death on the cross, nobody in the whole world stood any chance of being redeemed or saved.

Consequently, suffering in solidarity with the crucified Jesus provided the greatest hope of being saved. Suffering and holiness became strange bedfellows. The more one suffered the better one's chances of winning the spiritual battle. Suffering for its own sake, however, was strongly admonished.

I don't recall any one event or experience whereby I began to question what gradually I came to understand as a substantial perversion of faith. I do recall being introduced to a seminal work that articulated more clearly than I ever could the transpersonal understanding toward which I was being lured. I am alluding to the book *Saving Paradise*, a history of the cross in the ancient Christian world, authored in 2008 by American scholars Rita N. Brock and Rebecca Parker. Many churches today are adorned with a crucifix, highlighting the cruel and torturous suffering that Jesus underwent in his passion and death. Emblematic of what Jesus suffered for us, to redeem us from our sinful condition, this commonly used depiction of the death of Jesus is meant to remind us of our sin and call us to repentance to make up to Jesus for the cruel sufferings we caused him to endure. In the past, this left many people feeling even more guilt-ridden and unworthy.

What many Christians do not realize is that this type of crucifix—with the focus on the tortured, emaciated Jesus hanging on it—is very much an invention of the second Christian millennium and largely unknown for the first thousand years of Christendom. In the words of Brock and Parker, "It took Jesus 1,000 years to die."[56] The oldest evidence for this frequently used crucifix is that of the Gero Cross, in the Cathedral in Cologne, usually dated to 965 CE. Throughout the first Christian millennium, the cross adopted by Christians was typically that of an exalted risen Jesus, a glorified Christ, reigning over the world. No emphasis on torture and suffering, of the type depicted in Mel Gibson's *The Passion of The Christ*, where Jesus is flogged for approximately forty minutes, while the Sermon on the Mount is reduced to forty seconds.

The church historian Robin Jensen describes the change of focus as follows:

> Before the tenth or eleventh century, both Eastern and Western depictions typically refrained from showing Jesus as suffering physical agony and death. They tended to present Christ as vigorously alive....By the Middle Ages, images of the crucifixion had evolved from showing Christ as a living and victorious hero to a suffering and dying victim.[57]

What brought about the change? Two factors come to the fore.

a) *1095:* Pope Urban II instructs the Crusaders that they are to wear images of a tortured crucified Christ as they go to do battle with the infidels—presumably as a warrant for the torture of others and a validation for themselves in case they ended up being tortured.

b) *1097:* the publication of St. Anselm's book, *Cur Deus Homo?* (*Why Did God Become Human?*), outlining the first formal version of what in our time has come to be known as the doctrine of atonement.

From this time on, suffering for the sake of suffering becomes central to the notion of Christian salvation and redemption, with the historical Jesus upheld as the paradigmatic victim, whose violent death and suffering arrested the power of sin and opened the gates of heaven for sinful creatures. And those who suffered most were the ones who stood the best chance of inheriting eternal life in heaven.

Throughout the thirteenth and fourteenth centuries we can trace artistic and archaeological evidence for the growing popularity of the crucified imagery, with the wine in the chalice (at Eucharist) being ever more closely identified with the blood of Christ, exemplified in artistic images of blood coming from the side of Jesus and pouring into a chalice. With these devotional elements, the transpersonal fades into the background, as a new problematic personalism comes to the fore.

With the growing emphasis of dying with Jesus on the cross, *paradise* came to be understood in a whole new way. It referred to fulfillment with God in a life hereafter, far away from this earthly vale of tears contaminated by sin and human deviation. In the power of the crucified Christ, through consistent devotion to the cross and a readiness to suffer like Christ did, we could prepare ourselves for that eventual escape from the misery of this earthly condition to the fulfillment of life eternal in the paradise of heaven. Even from a personal viewpoint, this was only a partial resolution; it was the soul that would be saved, not the whole person.

Christians have long assumed that paradise has meant the same thing right through the two thousand years of Christendom, but not so! For the first thousand years it had a very different meaning. To quote Brock and Parker, "Paradise was the dominate image of early Christian sanctuaries,…first and foremost this world permeated and blessed by the Spirit of God."[58] The fulfillment of life with God in paradise was not understood as an escape from this earthly vale of tears (that belongs to the second millennium) but through an integrated relationship with the natural world, accompanied by a personal and interpersonal commitment to making the world a better place for all beings, human and nonhuman alike.

A substantial part of the evidence for this claim is that of the frescoes of the Roman catacombs in which we find few if any images of a crucifixion, or of a God standing in judgment, but an abundance of images from the natural world, luscious landscapes, inhabited with birds, animals, and humans in harmonious peace. Consequently, those that were martyred in Rome and commemorated in the catacombs did not opt for martyrdom in order to escape to eternal life hereafter but rather because they saw the sacrifice of their lives as a contribution to bringing about heaven on earth. They died in their service of God's creation, not to escape from it.[59]

Because of the loss, or suppression, of this transpersonal perspective of the paschal journey, we inevitably ended up with a misplaced understanding of the resurrection of Jesus as well. This ensues in a rather different understanding in the Eastern Orthodox Church from that in the West, a topic explored by John and Sarah Crossan and outlined in their inspiring monograph, *Resurrecting Easter*, in which they write: "In the first Christian millennium, both the individual and the universal tradition were prevalent; either could have become the Easter vision for all of Christianity. Not so in its inimical second millennium. The West chose individual imagery and the East retained universal iconography.... In the East's universal resurrection tradition, Christ arises and humanity rises along with him, by him, through him."[60]

The Cross of Creation

As a Christian people we have been subjected to several spiritual distortions, perhaps none more serious than the misrepresentation of the cross and the pernicious ways in which it has been used to keep people subdued in guilt and unworthiness. While acknowledging its importance for the comfort and strength of the unfortunate millions like Martha in Zambia, we must now acknowledge how seriously it has displaced the empowerment that Jesus modelled and delivered (in his life) for all Christians. And that empowering deliverance was intended not merely for humans but for all earthly creatures who suffer unjust cruelty.

To the best of my knowledge, Elizabeth Johnson's book *Creation and the Cross* (2018) is one of the first theological attempts to situate our theology of the cross (and Good Friday) in a more transpersonal context.[61] Crucifixion in our world today is first and foremost a cosmic and planetary reality. A great deal of human anguish, pain, and trauma results directly from the meaningless suffering the earth itself has to endure—largely because of reckless human interference. We lost our capacity to relate with creation in the context of paradise. We have become so disconnected from the sacredness of creation that we live our lives with a kind of inorganic alienation that is central to most of our pain and suffering.

The paschal journey for our time is to die to our anthropocentric preoccupation with control and usurpation of earth's resources for our own selfish benefit and to rise anew to a more convivial, integrated coexistence with the Gaian planet, the living earth itself. This is not some utopian escape from toil and suffering but rather a more enlightened way to embrace the suffering and healing that are endemic to creation at large.

Central to this shift of focus is an acknowledgment and integration of the paradoxical nature of creation, as outlined in chapter four. Once we begin to acknowledge that death and resurrection belong to creation at large, and did not begin merely with Jesus of Nazareth, it changes our outlook on everything. Not merely does it lead us to a different and deeper understanding of our Christian faith—outlined in the present chapter—but it brings us home to that deeper transpersonal identity so critical to the times in which we now live.

Modern technology promises us a world where one day human aging will be arrested, disease and death will cease to exist, and the perfect machine will bring an end to human struggle and drudgery. It is a delusory myth that strongly appeals to scientific futurists of our time but robs millions of people of more realistic hope. Christianity has its own version of this utopian myth: the lamb and the lion will lie down together (Isaiah 11:6). And all the nasty stuff will somehow be changed and transformed. Have no fear, *it is never going to happen.* And if perchance it ever did, it would be the greatest apocalyptic disaster creation would ever know.

Creation cannot survive, and less so thrive, without its dark side, its universal paschal journey. There is a quality of destruction, decay, and death that is essential to creation's flourishing. Without this downside there can never be evolutionary breakthroughs. Even Jesus himself endured the darkness, not merely in his death but primarily in his life, in his courageous prophetic challenges to the powers-that-be, as he pursued justice and empowerment for the marginalized people of his day, while also seeking eco-justice for the oppression meted out to the land itself. It is because Jesus gave his life so fully and unstintingly to this liberating and empowering transformation that he was eventually captured and crucified. The system could not tolerate him any longer.

The empowerment he was instigating became too much of a threat to the imperial and religious powers of the day.[62]

Jesus did not die for our sins (the atonement theory).[63] Jesus was killed because he was such an empowering prophet (the kingdom of God vision). He was crucified, which was a death meted out to subversives who posed a threat to the prevailing powers.

The transpersonal invitation, therefore, is to embrace life, darkness, suffering, struggle, breakthrough, and flourishing—the whole lot—with the fullness of our lives. And it is not merely life at the human level but that which pertains to the energizing and empowering web, to which we all belong at both cosmic and planetary levels.

In concluding her book *Creation and the Cross*, Elizabeth Johnson resituates the paschal journey in this expansive context:

> The cross of Christ brings this infinitely merciful love into a different kind of personal intimacy with the pain and death of creatures.... Together with the resurrection from which it cannot be separated, the cross anchors divine saving love historically in the flesh of the world's evolving life. In its light we see that the saving mercy accompanies all creatures in the world's beautiful, terrible journey through time to final fulfillment.... A theology of accompaniment sees God's redeeming action always present and active in the service of the flourishing of a world that is currently suffering reversals and death in a horrific way.[64]

The Way Ahead

Elsewhere in the same book Johnson writes: "The saving God became a human being, who was part of the wider human community, which shares the membrane of life with other creatures, all made from cosmic material, and vulnerable to death and disintegration."[65]

This quote indicates very directly where transpersonal empowerment takes us. Representing the human face of God, we are called afresh to embrace the challenge of becoming fully human. This cannot be done in individual isolation, however, but only through community that embraces all the creatures constituting with us the web of life. And within that planetary evolving process, paradox is always at work.

Indeed, deprived of that paradox, life would lack luster, ingenuity, and freedom. A predetermined world in which everything would evolve without struggle, pain, or suffering, would be quite a bland place and in all probability could not be capable of evolving the diverse, complex life-forms we know today, including our own species. Paradoxically, it would seem we inhabit the best of all possible worlds!

The crucial point, of course, is that we do not merely inhabit the universe. We are co-creators, participants in a complex creative process, and for the greater part we learn as we go along. Martha in Zambia had reached a cruel, painful juncture where the future looked very grim. All she could afford to learn was how to muster the basic courage to arise to the dark and frightening dawn of each day.

Until, that is, empowering grace came to her rescue, through the activists who risked so much so that Martha—and millions like her—could also regain some sense of being co-creators in a future worth living for. She may still be doing her rosaries, novenas, and devotions, but no longer pleading in desperation to a distant God, but now in gratitude to the God who liberates and empowers in the courageous endeavors of those who go the extra mile, the prophets that deliver enduring hope.

CHAPTER EIGHT

When the Able-Bodied Ruled the World

I've long thought of old age as a time when all that's left is to tell the truth—trying to remember to tell it in love. It's liberating to be at a point where I no longer need to posture or pretend because I no longer feel a need to prove anything to anyone.

—Parker J. Palmer.

In the Indian Ocean tsunami of December 26, 2004, many lives were lost and huge structural damage ensued. But one small indigenous group, virtually unknown in the wider world at that time, survived the terrible onslaught of that day. They opted to befriend a paradox exploding all around them and emerged as winners. Here is their story.

On the islands and coastal region of the Andaman Sea, on the west coast of Thailand, dwell a little-known indigenous group, the Moken tribe, sometimes described as the Morgan fisherfolk. This Austronesian ethnic group, numbering no more than three thousand members, maintain a nomadic, sea-based culture. Scientists have discovered that their children can see like dolphins down to seventy-five feet and that this improbable skill can be learned by any child.

As they gathered for breakfast on the morning of December 26, 2004, several members of the group noticed that the seawaters had receded to levels rarely seen, and fishes were popping up and down like toy figures in a carnival game, striving to survive. Gathering for breakfast, they invoked the wisdom of the elders as they detected that nature was out of balance and wondered how they should respond.

The elders advised that in a short time those receded waters would return with a momentous and highly destructive force. The group took preemptive action, gathering as much as they could of their meager belongings and headed for higher ground where they knew they would be safe.

On the way up, they met some Western tourists heading for the seafront. Unable to speak English, they urged the Westerners not to go down, but to little avail. As they went down, the tourists were trapped in the untimely waves and killed. A fortunate few scrambled their way back to higher ground and eventually reconnected with the Moken people. It was one of those lucky ones who told this story to the Western media.

Widely regarded as a primitive, ignorant group of people (they have little access to formal education), the Morgan fisherfolk are endowed with a wisdom that not only has survival value but also gives them access to the natural world to a degree that most Westerners have lost entirely. Perhaps more significant was the simple but profound discernment they did on that precarious morning. The God they knew to be right there in the living energy of creation—the throes of a paschal journey—itself spoke deeply in their hearts, empowering them to see beneath waves of fear and act with a wisdom that surely must challenge the most sublime knowledge any of us claim to have.

The lesson is as simple as it is profound. When we encounter the great paradoxes of creation, we must learn to flow with them. Don't resist them. If you choose to battle with them, you lose. Befriend the paradox, so that the paradox can befriend you—and be open to receiving that paradoxical wisdom from a range of different sources!

The Cult of the Able-Bodied

Our Western world, and the imperial values we have spread elsewhere, has little time for primitive people, their closeness to nature, and their incredible wisdom in engaging the paschal journeys of life. We cherish the able-bodied, the healthy and strong, those who make money (and spend it), those who can battle and win within the power dynamics of our brutally competitive world.

Primitive people are no good at that quality of engagement, but neither are those living with disability, those who are ethnically marginalized, and a range of others. And let's not forget the elderly who present a novel challenge in the West today and in other parts of the planet as well. Hidden beneath the veneer of invisibility is a surging phenomenon, a kind of cultural resurrection that requires urgent and creative response. From the demise of the able-bodied, whose destiny is becoming ever more precarious, the *wise elder* insinuates the cracks in the patriarchal system. The ones we would like to get rid of are waiting at the gate. And that gate we cannot keep locked anymore!

Here are the statistics, the imminent upsurge awaiting our attention and discernment. In 2017, there were an estimated 962 million people, aged sixty or over, spread throughout the world, comprising 13 percent of the global population. The population aged sixty or above is growing at a rate of about 3 percent per year. Currently, Europe has the greatest percentage of population aged sixty or over (25 percent). We now know that rapid aging will occur in other parts of the world as well, so that by 2050 all regions of planet Earth, except for Africa, will have nearly a quarter or more of their populations at age sixty and above. The number of older persons in the world is projected to be 1.4

billion in 2030 and 2.1 billion in 2050. It is expected that this figure will rise to 3.1 billion in 2100.

Globally, the number of persons aged eighty or over is projected to triple by 2050, from 137 million in 2017 to 425 million in 2050. By 2100 it is expected to increase to 909 million, nearly seven times its value in 2017. Already in 2020, the World Health Organization estimates that the number of people aged sixty years and older is outnumbering children younger than five years old. By 2030, one out of every five persons in the United States will have reached retirement age (sixty-five).

With this global aging profile we are approaching a cultural shift of enormous magnitude. Our thriving social and economic prosperity flourishes on the assumption that we will continue to have able-bodied people who will keep up our cultural and competitive momentum. Virtually every government in the world still assumes that there will be a continuous and consistent emergence of young labor to keep the world afloat. Despite the advances in technology that have significantly reduced the reliance on human labor, we still look to the energy and vitality of young minds and vigorous bodies to sustain the wheels of our capitalistic-driven world order.

Facing Our Aging Reality

The reader may wonder why I am introducing this strange topic into an autobiographical narrative. Is it apprehension and anxiety about my own aging process, which, admittedly, does concern me? I first developed an interest in this subject some twenty years ago, upon noting that the vast majority of participants in my workshops and retreats were those of older years, many in their seventies and eighties. It was in response to those encounters, and the intriguing questions arising, that I began to develop my interest in adult faith formation.

The older I get, the more convinced I am that the gentrification of our species is a prime example of the paschal journey at work in the twenty-first century. It requires and deserves all the discerning wisdom we can muster.

The Dreaded Aging Process

Coming to terms with an aging population is a dreaded prospect for nations and humans alike. Such is the widespread perception that older people are a cultural irrelevancy, nonproductive in monetary terms, a drain on the health system, a burden in terms of maintenance and care, they become the victims of a perverse unexamined prejudice. Our entire economic system is tilted in favor of young, able-bodied, productive agents. Our culture measures success and progress in terms of human prowess, with the ability to accumulate wealth as an underlying driving force.

Consequently, older people are sidelined in cultural terms and can easily begin to internalize a sense of personal and cultural uselessness. Deterioration in health and general well-being can absorb much of their time and energy and, in some cases, eat into their financial savings. Religiously—for those who retain some sense of religious belonging—the emphasis tends to be on preparation for death and the need to be ready to render an account to God. A great deal is piled up against our older people. Their personal worth and substantial giftedness is often ignored, bypassed, or suppressed.

As already indicated, our culture of mass production and fierce economic competitiveness tends to view older people in a negative light. Consequently, world governments pay scant attention to the global aging process outlined above. Neither governments nor money-makers are interested. No matter how compelling the evidence is—and it is undeniably persuasive—there is extensive denial around the global ageing issue. With the decreasing numbers of younger people available for "work," some governments are trying to move the retirement age further up the line (usually not beyond the age of seventy). While they note the decline in younger workers, they are simply not acknowledging the real issue, namely, that the world population is growing older and will continue to do so.

Implications for a Senior Culture

As a psychological defense mechanism, denial tends to embody a deeper psychic resistance, often based on unarticulated fears. This can be true of the person facing decline or death (as indicated in the research of the renowned psychologist Elizabeth Kübler-Ross) but also at the more systemic and cultural levels. If the policymakers of our world were to acknowledge the demographic shift to a rapidly increasing older population, several key contemporary values would come under new scrutiny. How can we sustain a culture of fierce competition without a cohort of young able-bodied people? And if we can't sustain it, what happens to our patriarchal prowess invested in big business and mega-corporations?

And the fears go much deeper. What will happen to our cherished masculine values for power and domination? And what will happen to our salacious advertising, sponging off the gullibility of youth and their passion to keep up with prevailing fashions—something that older people are not much interested in. And what of our political institutions when the dominant voter becomes an older citizen?

With the shift to a predominantly older culture, substantial changes lie afoot. These are poorly understood, because researchers, also influenced by cultural bias, tend not to look too closely at what these future trends might involve. Cultural historian Theodore Roszak bravely, and almost single-handedly, predicted the long-term prognosis: *it will be wise elders, and not younger people, who will drive our future civilization.* And the impetus will be already obvious by the middle of the twenty-first century.

The American educator and activist Parker J. Palmer, in his book *Gravity and Grace: On the Brink of Everything*, provides an inspiring and challenging read on how old age can be revisioned along the horizon of generativity rather than stagnation:

> Looking around at the shared world, its suffering and its promise, I see the courage with which so many live in service of the human possibility. Old age is no time to hunker down, unless disability demands it. Old age is just another word for nothing left to lose, a time of life to take bigger risks on behalf of the common good.... We need to reframe ageing as a passage of discovery and engagement, not decline and inaction.[66]

And for Palmer, the grace of living well—and generatively—in older years is to transcend the frenzied drivenness that so militates against more reflective and discerning ways of being. All over our troubled world today, people need to die to overactivism and rise to contemplative solitude, for which the American Trappist monk Thomas Merton is often cited as an inspiring source. Palmer advocates this interiority as an essential feature for growth in becoming a wise elder.

Unfortunately, the derogatory culture we inhabit condemns many older people to being "dead before our time," thus inhibiting, if not totally undermining, the transition into becoming wise elders. In some cases, older people, frightened and disturbed by the loss of traditional values and mores, become entrenched and defensive around inherited ways of being. It largely depends on educational opportunities, and this becomes another major hurdle for the dominant cultures of our contemporary world. With so many demands on maintaining our schools (for youth) and universities, the challenge of diverting resources to the older sectors is an issue that few if any governments have thus far addressed.

Meanwhile, older folks themselves are picking up the baton and taking their own initiatives. Many of these learners are over seventy years of age. And when these older people embrace afresh their intellectual development (not to be confused with academic achievement), frequently a spiritual awakening also takes place (another development that has been poorly researched). This does not necessarily mean a return to religion, but the development of a more altruistic, compassionate view of life, often accompanied by what James Fowler identified several years ago as a new universal consciousness.

From the Personal to the Transpersonal

This is the religious stereotype of the old person: Now that you cannot earn money to keep the economy going and may be a burden on the health system due to increased medical needs, the time has come to give up your worldly ways, make your peace with God and with the world, and prepare to meet your God in judgment.

Of course, we adopt a similar set of dismissive and prejudicial attitudes toward a range of other people: our indigenous sisters and brothers, asylum seekers and refugees, people with disability, unemployed people, those who have been incarcerated. In a culture where we are expected to be politically correct, we say and do the right thing, but beneath the surface we hold a range of judgmental attitudes.

My concern in this chapter is that of elderly people, rapidly becoming a major economic and political force in our world. I also support the view that they are likely to become significant spiritual catalysts for the twenty-first century. This new rising (resurrection) embodies a set of religious features very different from mainline religion. We are into the sphere of the transpersonal, particularly its mystical horizons.

When James Fowler first outlined his religious approach to life stages, he identified this older group as the universalists.[67] Fowler regarded this life stage as a deeply reflective time open to new cosmic vision and the appropriation of a more global sense of spirituality. Susan Cook-Greuter endorses this insight in what she describes as the postautonomous stage. It is characterized by two phases: first, *the construct-aware phase* in which people review more critically their inherited linguistic and metaphorical concepts, and *the unitive phase,* experienced as a transcendence of the subject-object polarity along with a deepening sense of being at one with everything in creation.

In the closing decades of the twentieth century many people were offered the option of early retirement (from fifty-five onward), and since many of these people were still healthy and active (in every sense), opportunities were sought to reemploy their talents and resources. One significant outcome, already referenced, is the emergence of the University of the Third Age (popularly known as UTA or U3A). Today this educational facility, reserved to the over-fifties, accommodates an estimated ten million people in the Americas, Europe, Australia, India, and China. The popular prejudicial perception of older people being unemployable, nonproductive, and a drain on financial and health resources quickly changed, although much awareness-raising still needs to be done.

Beyond early retirement, a further life stage requires renewed attention in our time, namely, those over the age of seventy. In religious terms people in this subgroup are assumed to be in declining health and are thus admonished to do penance and prepare to meet God in death and judgment. In the Hindu faith, the elderly devotee is even encouraged to leave home and family and assume a life of greater austerity and simplicity, stages known as *vanaprastha* (forest recluse) and *sanyasi* (complete renunciation).

In the 1970s, a revitalization of the notion of the wise elder came to the fore, with Fowler's characteristic of *universality* getting the attention of various researchers. Despite its scholarly limitations, the pioneering work of James Fowler still remains seminal. Initially a Western development, it has now become much more widespread, with implications for the global consciousness of our time and particularly its spiritual (mystical) implications.

Two critical factors come into play here. The first, already noted, is what Theodore Roszak calls the longevity revolution, with those of older age becoming not merely numerically stronger in population terms but also a determining political and economic force as I shall indicate shortly. Second, the information explosion has had, and will continue to have, a major influence on these older people. While they don't exhibit the dexterity of the young nor their fascination with modern information technology, they imbibe the newly emerging consciousness for *interconnectedness, wholeness, and universality.* They become curious and eager to learn more; their intuition is freshly awakened, and their imaginations are stretched in the direction of ever-expanding awareness, characteristic of evolving consciousness in our time with some significant theological implications.

Because our dominant culture is so anti-aging (except for the technological compulsion toward perpetual youthfulness and the end of dying) and largely dismissive of the elderly as useless and nonproductive, only limited research has gone into the alternative phenomenon I am highlighting. I know from personal experience that an alternative elder culture is arising (rapidly and universally) and that in a matter of a few decades it will exert substantial influence on our global value systems.

We are rapidly approaching the critical threshold when in several Western countries the elderly will become (a) the dominant voters, much more critically aware of political policies, and not easily lured to support the inherited party system, and (b) the leading purchasers, whose buying options will not be determined by popular fashion or commercial spin but by aesthetic, ecological, and more responsible values. Thanks to the preponderance of these older consumers, sustainability in values and practices is likely to expand significantly, requiring major changes in marketing, advertising, and consumer practice.

My interest in this new subgroup is mainly spiritual and religious in nature. These elders (which I define as over fifty-five) come mainly from a formal religious background, tend to be well educated, and often belong to the middle-to-upper class. They question almost everything in their inherited faith, however, and wish to stretch spiritual understandings far beyond conventional religious belief. In their expansive vision they seek to outgrow the dualistic split between sacred and secular; for them sacredness is universal and predates religion by millions of years.

The Elder Take on Mysticism

The morbid feelings we often adopt in our regard for the elderly have no place in the reconstruction I am offering in this chapter. Those of us who have studied scholastic philosophy will be acquainted with the dictum: action follows thought. If we interpret the phrase broadly, regarding thinking not merely as a rational mental exercise but as a deeply reflective process, then the quality of the ensuing action will be determined by the quality of thought and perception.

Because of their universal ways of seeing and understanding, wise elders serve an important spiritual function in our time. They are guardians of the mystical, which is foundational to what I describe in this book as the transpersonal. In a world inundated by rational discourse, and to a degree that seeks to dismiss and ridicule all other modes of perception and knowledge, the wise elders represent an alternative way of inhabiting cosmic and planetary space. Their approach is more gentle, noninvasive, and holistic. Their mode of engagement is collaborative rather than competitive, value-centered rather than commercially driven. At heart they are universalists rather than confined by ideology, creed, or culture.

Theirs is an engaged mysticism, seeking not to transcend the world to some idyllic utopian life beyond but to become more deeply immersed in the quantum-entangled creation of the here-and-now. Consider this description from the theologian Leonardo Boff:

> Mysticism is life apprehended in its radicalism and extreme density. Existence is endowed with gravity, buoyancy, and depth when this is conceived and known appropriately. Mysticism always leads to the transcendence of all limits. It persuades us to examine other aspects of things than those we know and to suspect that reality is more than a mere structure concealing the realm of the absurd and the abyss, which can strike fear and anguish into our hearts.... The mystic is not detached from history but committed to it as transformation, starting from a nucleus of transcendent meaning and a minimal utopian dimension which, in as much as it is religious, enables the mystic to be more perceptive than anybody else.[68]

"More perceptive than anybody else" provides a central clue to the role our wise elders play—and are more likely to be playing—in the evolutionary world of our time. Amid the frenzied activity of our age, our culture needs pockets of pregnant silence, where depth and breadth become more transparent and the potential for empowering meaning becomes clearer.

Our wise elders are already pursuing these new cultural and spiritual horizons, but our dominant culture either cannot see or, more likely, does not wish to see. Elders tend to be attracted to the organic and a process approach to life. They embrace the flow and move within its momentum. They tend not to carry the fear of death and dying, so widespread in our world. Consequently, they also hold in a more integrated way the several paradoxes of the paschal journey.

In making these generalized observations, I am acutely aware of my white, Western status, where several of our wise elders come from wealthy, well-educated backgrounds. They have the privilege of long, fruitful lives, have seen their families reared, and enjoy the many affirmations of their grandchildren. They have cleared their debts and tend to live quite comfortably. In the eyes of others, they can afford to be philanthropic, go to conferences, and avail themselves of resources for spiritual nourishment.

Millions around our world do not have this luxury, condemned to the daily grind of trying to survive amid warfare, violence, poverty, and exploitation at the hands of mega-corporations. This is indeed a cruel dilemma that cries out for justice. The German liberation theologian Dorothee Soelle is one of the few people who has attempted an integration across this deeply disturbing cultural and spiritual chasm. She describes the coming together of mysticism and justice-making in our human resolve to break through the painful divide outlined above:

> The basis of spiritual renewal is not the guilt feelings that frequently arise in sensitized individuals in rich industrial societies. Instead, it is a crazy mysticism of becoming empty that reduces the real misery of the poor and diminishes one's own slavery. Becoming empty or "letting go" of the ego, possession, and violence is the precondition for the creativity of transforming action.[69]

Elders and the Paschal Journey

As our world population grows older and seniors become the cultural catalysts calling forth a wider desire for more sustainable living, wise elders will become much more visible at a transnational level. That will confront all humans with the challenge to live in more sustainable ways. For some it will feel like a dying to privilege and power, but to others, hopefully it will be the rolling back of the tombstone, leaving indeed a frightening gaping hole but paradoxically imbued with empowering presence of risen hope.

Can we get there without a major crisis? That is the million-dollar question for which none of us has a ready answer. We can draw some hope from the fact that as a seven-million-year-old species we have been through several major crises and we have come through them—not without major adjustments, of course. In our genes we know not merely how to survive but how to thrive. Indeed, that capacity for flourishing is the hidden goal of every paschal journey.

At the very least all of us can make a perceptual shift that will help us to break through the still destructive dualisms that continue to plague our world. The wisdom of the elders is not an exclusive endowment of the rich, powerful, able-bodied, and well-educated but can also be discerned among those with disability, the refugees, social outsiders, indigenous people, and the Gospel-rejects labelled as the "prostitutes, sinners and tax-collectors."

Contemporary technology has delivered and is delivering the possibilities of a much more interconnected world. It also provides significant breakthroughs for the eradication of poverty and disease. But it is not without its shadow, a new insatiable and compulsive drive to create a perfect world devoid of the great paradox: technology aims at a perfect world, but it is a quality of perfection that is deeply alien to a paradoxical creation that can neither survive nor flourish without open-endedness, untidiness, vulnerability, suffering that awakens compassion, the freedom to err, the reality of human limitation. Were it a perfect world, there would be no room for freedom and creativity.

In the context of the present work, technology's desire to get rid of death is the most disturbing of all. As highlighted throughout this book, death is an integral dimension of all organic life, the evolutionary complement to life's growth and flourishing. If we eliminate death, we will have automatically destroyed life (at least as we know it in the contemporary universe).

Our elders are well aware of living through the sunset years of their lives. Those among them who inspire us with their wisdom and vision are acutely aware of the provisionality of the human condition. This does not, however, hinder them from being proactive and creative in seeking to bring about a better world. They desire it for their children and grandchildren. Deep in their hearts they are imbued with a transpersonal vision, stretching beyond the merely human, as they embrace care for our common earthly home and the welfare of all that sustains and enriches the universal web of life.

The Death and Resurrection of Catholicism

> *So, knowing Jesus implies, of necessity, a gradual setting free from any sense of tribal belonging....I think it is particularly sad when Catholics turn belonging to the Church into a sectarian belonging, into a definable cultural group with a clearly marked inside and outside, and firm ideas to who belongs outside. Of such people, it can be said that they do not go into the Kingdom of Heaven.*
>
> —James Alison

Throughout much of my childhood and much of my early life, one sacrament loomed large, namely, the Eucharist. Of course, we never called it that, and to this day, it is not the word that most Catholics use. Instead, they talk about going to Mass or attending church. Mass tends to be perceived as a duty and an obligation, without which salvation (in a life hereafter) cannot be obtained. And the celebration of Eucharist is not possible without an ordained priest, endowed with the divine power to bring Jesus down upon the altar, so that the people are nourished as passive recipients of salvific grace.

As a seminarian, I remember well my eucharistic theology (by a Jesuit professor) that left me in no doubt about the fact that it is the Holy Spirit of God that informs and empowers every eucharistic celebration. The "change" of the eucharistic elements (bread and wine) results not from the magical words of the priest but from the *epiclesis*, the double invocation of the Holy Spirit, first upon the elements and later upon the gathered worshiping community. "We ask you to send your Holy Spirit to change these gifts of bread and wine." The agent of change is not the priest but the Holy Spirit of God.

Despite that very clear and informed theology, I went on to celebrate Eucharist—for at least twenty years—before taking seriously what I had learned in seminary. Such was the influence of the widespread belief that it is *the power of the priest* that makes the difference and that without a priest there can be no Eucharist.

Another issue that never even dawned on me was the fact that the celebration of Eucharist was reserved to males. Only men could become priests! I faintly recall the unquestioned logic: only the twelve were at the Last Supper, and Eucharist is based totally on that special sacrificial meal that Jesus shared with the twelve apostles on the night before he died.

Twenty or, perhaps, thirty years on, I began to realize that Jesus shared several meals with his followers, most, it seems, with a nefarious group consisting of outcasts, sinners, and prostitutes. There was no allusion to the kind of preparation deemed to be so essential in my early formative years: make sure you are not in a state of sin, and if in any doubt, make a perfect act of contrition! Nor were any of the participants asked to proclaim their unworthiness as occurs at a nauseating rate in the current translation of the Roman Missal.

How we ended up where we are with an understanding of Eucharist that Jesus would scarcely recognize would require a historical analysis well beyond the purview of this book. In all the Christians churches, we are at a *kairos* moment (sacred time) in the evolutionary understanding of Eucharist. Originally, Eucharist was an ordinary meal, totally inclusive, empowering, liberating, and engaging the participants in a nourishing ritual in which they knew God to be intimately close and incarnationally real.[70]

Books and websites by Roman Catholicism apologists will often emphasize that the Catholic church began with Jesus or, more precisely, with the Acts of the Apostles. The same sources go on to specify the centrality of Rome to the emergence of Catholicism and, crucially, the papacy as the embodiment on earth of divine power and validation and, therefore, the only reliable guarantor of the truth of faith.

What began in early Christian times was the Christian church, of which the Roman Catholic denomination is one offshoot, albeit numerically the strongest at the present time. Catholicism, as we know it today, has departed significantly from the Gospel vision of Jesus, as indeed have other major denominations. Patriarchal power is the issue on which all Christian churches have deviated from their original inspiration. That deviation first transpired in the fourth century with Constantine's endorsement of Christianity, a religion he molded very much along the lines of domination and patriarchal control.[71] And for Roman Catholicism, there was a second major deviation, the Council of Trent in the sixteenth century.

Trent's Petrified Defense

The Council of Trent began in 1545 and ended eighteen years later in 1563. Regarded by many clerical church historians as one of the most important and auspicious councils of the church, it marked a rupture within Christianity that has had deleterious consequences down to our own day. The council was a petrified reaction to the perceived attack of the Protestant Reformation. The council made no attempt to understand or reconcile the grievances of the Protestants. In fact, it set out to criminalize all such criticism. While the council did move to eliminate some of the abuses that had stirred up the Reformation (for example, selling of indulgences and clerical corruption), it re-created a church claiming a monopoly of power that seriously undermined the empowerment of the Christian Gospel.

Clerical power became a major issue at the Council of Trent, taking on a central importance also for the other denominations that emerged around the same time: Lutherans, Calvinists, and others. For Catholicism, it was very much a panic reaction. Feeling embarrassed and ashamed by the perceived betrayal of Protestantism, the church resolved that it would do everything possible to ensure that such a departure from truth would never again happen.

To that end, Trent put in place a robust system of structure and regulation to safeguard the one and only truth, which the Catholic church alone could deliver. A key aspect of this system was to create a superior person-in-charge, who is best described by four key words: *male, white, celibate, cleric.*

Male: Faithful to Aristotle's anthropology, endorsed by St. Thomas Aquinas, only males are considered to be full human beings, with God-given rational intelligence. The other half, namely, females, cannot, and must not, be trusted with serious responsibilities for the future of the church.

White: At the time, the white Western world, which essentially means Europe, was regarded as the only civilized part of the planet. The colonization of other parts was already at work in the Americas and in subsequent centuries was to spread to other continents. The vision of Trent and colonization go hand-in-hand.

Celibate: Since God was viewed as asexual, those who truly represent God must be asexual as well. But there is a further nuance to the celibate state, denoting a quality of holiness equal to God himself. The priest has been granted a divine (or at least, semi-divine) status.

Cleric: Fundamentally, this means a quality of power equal to God himself. So, only a cleric is authorized to speak on God's behalf and to truly represent God on earth.[72]

Within this structure, no prospect of adult maturity among the people of God is tolerated. Even the privileged clerical few are themselves caught up in a tyrannical power game. Everybody ends up in codependent, dysfunctional relationships. In a sense, everybody is powerless, in a system that eventually will implode. It can be so tightly buttressed, however, that it can endure for centuries, eventually running out of energy and fragmenting in a rather meaningless decimation. Evidence for this corrosive fragmentation is visible in all the Christian denominations today. And several of the Christian denominations don't know what to do about it.

Popular Devotion

Those holding the power—the male, white, celibate clerics—enforced their power chiefly by perpetuating a form of devotionalism that kept people passive, feeling unworthy, obedient, and subservient. Such devotionalism flourished through various movements, one of the better known being that of Jansenism.[73] Original sin was highlighted as the central plight of all humanity, condemning humans to an enduring state of perversion and sin, which could be remedied only by penance and prayer, in the hope of making up to Jesus for his cruel sufferings (on the cross) caused by flawed humans.

One of the major problems with such devotions is that enough was never enough. The more penance one did, the more unworthy and inadequate one felt, and, therefore, one had to keep adding additional effort. Almost inevitably people began to internalize a tyrannical demanding God who could never be satisfied, a God that would never give the graces necessary for salvation unless we bombarded him day and night.

Such intense pleading with this highly manipulative, punitive God was done through repetitive prayers (for example, the rosary), novenas, fasting and other forms of bodily deprivation, pilgrimages, exaggerated use of statues and holy pictures, frequent attendance at church services, in obedience to the male, white, celibate clerics. In this way people were kept in perpetual childish immaturity, embracing a sense of faith with little scope for adult growth and development.

In the latter half of the twentieth century, many people in the West outgrew the codependency of such devotionalism and in several cases abandoned church practice completely. In other parts of the world, the devotions were integrated with popular fiestas and local community celebrations, and in that process the severity of the penitential practices was reduced considerably. In communities around the world where poverty and violence prevail, such devotional practices are still prevalent as people hope against hope that God will intervene and rescue them from their awful situations. By upholding and encouraging such devotional practices, instead of confronting on a practical level the systemic injustice and oppression of such peoples, both church and state often collude in making the situation tolerable for the people.

Heresy and Monolithic Truth

In the post-Tridentine church, any disagreement with, or deviation from, official church teaching automatically puts one beyond the pale.

There was no room for disagreement or for alternative opinion. There was no acknowledgment of the hugely diverse nature of faith that prevailed in early Christian times. There was only one truth and one way to knowing and appropriating truth, and that was through the teaching authority of the church.

Theologians were often mouthpieces for the hierarchy. Theology was strictly reserved to priests and those training for priesthood, a procedure that remained rigidly in place until the second half of the twentieth century. It began to loosen its grip around 1970, when an estimated 5 percent of all theologians in the Catholic church were laypeople; today we reckon it is in the region of 60 percent. During the post-Tridentine period, heresy was not merely about deviating from right doctrine. More significant, it denoted breaking the laws and rules in a church becoming ever more preoccupied with law and canonical regulations, all leading up to the promulgation of the *Code of Canon Law* in 1917. Law has always been a central feature of Christianity, but with a milder and less extensive application than what happened after the Council of Trent when a new legalistic momentum came to the fore, popularly known as the *Jus Novissimum* (newest law).

Marriage provides a valuable example. Before the Council of Trent, marriage was not a sacrament in the formal sense. There was a blessing of the union and concern from the church for the welfare of spouses and children, but a great deal was left to the people's own initiative in a culture characterized by trust and goodwill. After Trent we witness a gradual movement toward controlling every aspect of people's marital reality, to the present situation in which an estimated one-third of the *Code of Canon Law* is about marriage.

Altruism Indomitable

Despite the negative factors outlined thus far, suggesting that the post-Tridentine period was one of regression and growing legalism, an incarnational altruism also flourished extensively. Perhaps that will remind us that despite the cultural impositions from on high, the Spirit continues to breathe amid the chaos, particularly among those perceived to be the losers. In religious terms we note this in a range of countercultural movements flourishing throughout the post-Tridentine era.

On the religious front, one movement that has not received the attention it deserves is that of female religious congregations.

> In 1298, Pope Boniface VIII issued a decree, *Periculoso*, prescribing new and more rigorous standards for the enclosure of women Religious than the Western church had previously demanded.... The bull reflected current fears that women were inherently passionate and lusted after sexual fulfilment even more ardently than men. At the Council of Vienne in 1311, Pope Clement V extended the *Periculoso* to include Beguines, Tertiaries, and other less formally consecrated women. At a later date, Pope Pius V (1566–1572) declared solemn vows and strict papal enclosure to be essential to all communities of women religious.[74]

Such enclosure was never formally revoked, yet a new wave of female religious life emerged in the sixteenth and seventeenth centuries with such pioneering figures as Angela Merici, Louise de Marilac, Mary Ward, and Mary McKillop. They targeted the human and apostolic needs of the poor and marginalized, activating a range of services that were to evolve into the educational systems and health services we know today in many parts of the Western world.

Alongside the apostolic congregations of sisters, a range of charitable services also transpired, attending to the medical, social, and educational needs of people, particularly the very poor. Beyond a church with a public ascetical and legalistic image, there flourished a widespread active devotion, not focused on prayer and penance but on radiating the human face of Christ in compassionate love and empowering liberation. Few historical sources acknowledge this hidden resourcefulness, which sustained millions through pain and struggle.

This altruistic undercurrent, so profound and pervasive within Catholicism is elegantly captured by the American scripture scholar James Carroll, writing in *The Atlantic* in June 2019:

> Around the world there are more than 200,000 Catholic schools and nearly 40,000 Catholic hospitals and healthcare facilities, mostly in developing countries. The Church is the largest non-governmental organization on the planet, through which selfless women and men care for the poor, teach the unlettered, heal the sick, and work to preserve minimal standards of the common good. The world needs the Church of these legions to be rational, historically minded, pluralistic, committed to peace, a champion of the equality of women, and a tribune of justice.

Replacing the diseased model of the church with something healthy may involve, for a time, intentional absence from services or life on the margins—less in the pews than in the rearmost shadows. But it will always involve deliberate performance of the works of mercy: feeding the hungry, caring for the poor, visiting the sick, striving for justice. These can be today's chosen forms of the faith. It will involve, for many, unauthorized expressions of prayer and worship—egalitarian, authentic, ecumenical—having nothing to do with diocesan borders, parish boundaries, or the sacrament of holy orders.

Some years ago, the British theologian Tina Beattie captured the prevailing mood in this perceptive statement:

> The paradoxical nature of the Catholic tradition makes it resistant to the controlling logic of the modern world, and indeed to the controlling manoeuvring of the Catholic hierarchy. For the life of the Church is embodied not in the college of Cardinals, but in the hopes and visions, fears and sorrows, of those millions around the world whose faith finds expression in muddled expressions of desire and denial, where the body of Christ mingles with the touch and tingle, with the blood and semen, milk and mucus, of our ordinary human couplings and encounters in a Eucharistic community that scrambles our tiny boundaries of nation, kin and class, laws and creeds. The pontificating of cardinals and feminist theologians alike barely impinges upon this other Catholicism whose fecundity lies not in bearing babies for the Pope but in the stubborn persistence of Christ's maternal love for the world.[75]

It is indeed a wounded Church, as the sex scandals of the late twentieth century highlighted all too clearly. Unfortunately, the moralistic, and at times voyeuristic, analysis of the sexual abuse has deflected attention away from the critical paschal journey transpiring for the Catholic church on a global scale. This is the crucifixion of clericalism, and while safeguarding procedures need attention, and victims need to be embraced, these remedial actions will offer no long-term resolution (no "resurrection") till the prerequisite dying is first named and addressed. As many commentators have highlighted, the central issue is not the abuse of sex but the transgression of power. Nor is celibacy the problem; power is the problem. The day for the white celibate cleric is coming to an end, and, the clerical sex abuse is a central feature of this dark Calvary hour.

From the Personal to the Transpersonal

Throughout the post-Tridentine era, until about 1960, the primary concern of Catholic doctrine and governance was the redemption of human beings, more specifically, the salvation of their immortal souls. It was a very person-centered religion but embedded in a dangerously narrow anthropology.

In 1959, Pope John XXIII detected a serious malaise within the church and recommended that we open the ecclesiastical windows and let in some fresh air. What he had not anticipated was the strong evolutionary wind of the Spirit, which did a great deal more than clearing away the cobwebs; in the deliberations of Vatican II (1959–1964), it shifted "furniture" all over the place, to a degree that left many wondering if the church itself was not in danger of falling apart. Not surprisingly, therefore, two successive popes, John Paul II and Benedict XVI, tried to rein in the momentum of reform and managed to disrupt and even halt some much needed change.

But the Spirit had already broken lose. The 1960s inaugurated a waft of cultural shifts opening up new breakthroughs, many chaotic but, in the end, all creative. Even if Vatican II had never happened, the waves of change impacting the Catholic church today would have come about. These are evolutionary changes, whose deeper meaning has not yet been detected nor discerned. Fundamentally, they are theological in nature and transpersonal in their transformative power—and not without the proverbial mix of light and shadow! The following overview will give a sense of their evolutionary direction.

The Catholic Church Today

The Catholic church today consists of 1.3 billion members, over 99 percent of whom are nonclerical. In other words, priests, bishops, cardinals, right up to the pope together comprise less than 1 percent of the entire body. Why, then, is the Catholic church so preoccupied with the clerical dimension that comprises such a tiny part of the entire organism? Why do Catholics themselves, and the media, tend to judge the church by what goes on at the clerical institutional level? Surely, in the name of justice, apart entirely from truth, we need to shift the focus. The Catholic church is a people's church. How, and when, therefore, will we let the clericalism die so that the true church can rise up in resurrection empowerment?

Second, the demographic shift of recent decades requires even a more substantial paschal journey, dying in order to rise anew. In 1960, 66 percent of the Catholic population of the world lived in the white Western spheres (United States, Canada, Europe, Australia), which means 34 percent was resident in the South, predominantly in Central and South America. As we moved into the twenty-first century, we witnessed a rapid and marked shift from West to South, estimated in 2020 to be 80 percent in the South and merely 20 percent in the white Western world.

The one-time powerful, imperial church of the West is in serious decline, in fact facing terminal diminishment to a degree that very few Catholics are prepared to acknowledge. This is no mere demographic shift! I wager that God is in this movement, indeed might well be its propelling impetus. God wants this to happen. God's Spirit is the driving force within and behind it.

In every paschal journey there is an institutional death at work, a kind of a purification process necessary to clear out the old staid accumulations and empty out the structural containers so that they can be refilled with the new wine of the Spirit. A major challenge facing contemporary Catholicism is that the new wine of the South can't flow freely because catechetics and theological formation is largely of the old school. But let's not lose hope! If the Spirit is within this movement, then we are dealing with a messy, untidy revolution that cannot be halted.

This brings me to a third major shift. Ever since the Council of Trent, theology was strictly reserved to priests and priests-to-be (clerical students). Slowly that began to change in the mid-twentieth century, reaching a new threshold where an estimated 60 percent of all theologians in the Catholic church today are laypeople (mainly women), with priests comprising about 40 percent and on a downward curve. I acknowledge that some of the lay theologians are quite clerical in outlook and approach, but for the greater part the lay theologian brings a different perspective; she or he does theology in terms of the world and not merely the church. A different theological consciousness is awakening us to new life.

The lived experience and the structures through which we filter our experience will arise from the quality of our consciousness (thought and perception). With the current theological shift in the Catholic church from the cleric to the layperson, we can expect a significant departure from the former confessional theological approach to one that grounds our theological vision and hope within the emerging evolutionary consciousness of our time. Once again, a paschal journey is unfolding, a dying to a former consciousness and an awakening receptivity to a creation-centered theological synthesis.[76]

A church from the ground up—evolving amid much pain and confusion—will also embrace a very different kind of theology. This movement is already well underway and can be traced back to 1943, when Pope Pius XII issued the challenging document, *Divino Afflante Spiritu* (On the most opportune way to pursue biblical studies). In this document, the pope is asking Catholic scripture scholars not to rely solely on the Vulgate (the Latin Bible) but also to engage the ancient languages of Greek, Hebrew, and Aramaic. Effectively, the pope was requesting that literal interpretation of the Latin Bible should be superseded in favor of a deeper and more discerning analysis, arising from a more comprehensive acquaintance of older literary and cultural sources. The American Catholic scholar Raymond Brown described this document as the Magna Carta of Catholic biblical studies in the twentieth century.

From 1950 onward, thanks in part to the new guidelines issued by Pope Pius XII, the study of both scripture and theology began to move in a new direction. Faith seeking understanding was seen in a new light. The very foundations of the faith itself were no longer perceived to be static and monolithic. New strategies of understanding—how to engage with ancient texts—were invoked. Truth came to be seen as an ongoing process and not merely as a once-and-for-all deposit.

We Are Nature

In May 2015, Pope Francis issued his encyclical letter *Laudato Si'* (*On Care for our Common Home*), evidence that at last the Catholic church is catching up on the creation-centered message of the Gospel: "Nature cannot be regarded as something separate from ourselves or as a mere setting in which we live. We are part of nature, included in it and thus in constant interaction with it" (#139).

I suspect the originality of this statement has been missed by many readers and commentators. To the best of my knowledge this is the first papal document ever to echo such sentiments. It turns on its head the long dualistic split, the basis of so much devotional asceticism, so often highlighted in Christian spirituality. For the church throughout the centuries, the natural world was viewed as the harbinger of all that distracts us from the things of God, leading us into temptation and sin. It denoted the vale of tears from which one day we would hopefully escape to the supernatural realm of the afterlife.

After all this time, amid centuries of denunciation and renunciation, Pope Francis is inviting us to come back home to our true God-given nature as Earthlings. As such, we belong intimately to the clay from which we are formed, and our salvation is to be worked out in constant interaction with the earthly web of life and with all the other creatures who share the planetary home with us. This is truly revolutionary stuff, elegantly substantiated by the British ecological scientist Tom Oliver in his book *The Self Delusion*! This is a powerfully inspiring book that brings to life the overwhelming evidence contradicting the perception we have of ourselves as independent beings and illustrating in great detail, not merely our interdependence in the cosmic scheme of things, but the massive and urgent adjustments we need to make if we want to live more creatively and responsibly on this planet.

Strangely, this is actually the kind of organic faith that rank-and-file Catholics have known for a long time, just as I knew it amid the bioregional homestead of my early formative years. Perhaps this is the transpersonal depth that has sustained Catholics over many centuries, in spite of the fame and fervor of the hierarchical structure and in spite of the power-mongering pursued by the male, white, celibate clerics of Trent. As theologian Tina Beattie suggested in the quote above, there is indeed another Catholicism, and I suspect there always has been. Perhaps *Laudato Si'* is merely recovering what, in our mystical depths, we have always known. A scientific naturalist turned Catholic, Chet Raymo, might serve as an example of that latent, suppressed Catholic spirit:

> Immortality looms less large in the Catholic sensibility than in Protestantism. We Catholics are dreadfully attached to this world of water, wax, bread and wine, flesh and blood, incense, chrism, light and darkness—in short all those things the Reformers dismissed as idolatrous. We don't want to be raptured out of our bodies; if we are going to some other place we want to take our bodies with us.... I continue to hope that Catholic educators will resist the lapse into religious fundamentalism and become instead a shining example of the virtue so necessary for our common future—a love for the world as we empirically find it, and a sense that everything in it is holy.[77]

And critical to the discernment of our time is the confused state of priesthood itself. As indicated in chapter eight, ever since the Council of Trent in the sixteenth century we have been inundated with clericalism, and, correspondingly, we have seriously undermined the radical meaning of priesthood devoted to empowering service and meant to be devoid of all hankering after patriarchal power. That is the Calvary now engaging us. Clericalism is dying and will die out eventually.

What shape the resurrection will take has not yet been revealed. Very likely, it will involve a reclaiming of the empowering inclusivity at the heart of all Gospel meals. It has substantial implications for a renewal of Eucharist and indeed for all the sacraments. It will involve returning sacraments to the people, to whom they belong in the first place. That will require a further resurrection: people reclaiming their authentic creative adulthood, with the readiness to learn and internalize what empowering ritual (sacramentality) entails.

The early decades of the twenty-first century, throughout the Catholic church, have been a dark night of excruciating pain. As sex scandals rocked the church's integrity, its leaders fumbled and stumbled, not sure how to respond. This indeed was—and continues to be—a Calvary time, and I believe the worst is yet to come. What we are now witnessing is not merely a set of sexual deviations, linked to a gross abuse of clerical power. *It is the crucifixion of clericalism itself.* And after the death is duly registered, a funeral must take place, a challenge nobody in the Catholic faith community has yet even entertained.

It is foolhardy of me, or of anybody else, to speculate on what the ensuing resurrection will look like, but I don't think it will be a revival of priesthood along the lines we have long known. New structures of ecclesial leadership will certainly evolve, and I suspect they will be overtly lay in nature. The church of the people of God will rise from the proverbial ashes, and no doubt God will visit and empower the people once more.

I wager my faith that this new breakthrough will honor the ground-up faith long known to the Catholic people of God, who will rediscover the empowerment of the reign of God (the new companionship), not in a church cut off from the world, but in faith communities deeply grounded in nature itself. In our dream to save the world, we will discover anew the unconditional love of God calling us to be God's people walking our earthly pathway of grace and beauty.

CHAPTER TEN

Holding Integrity in a Liminal Impasse

> *For me, writing is not about gathering facts, wrapping them in lucid thoughts, then getting them down on the page. It begins by dropping deep into my not-knowing, and dwelling in the dark long enough for my eyes to adjust and start to see what's down there.*
>
> —Parker J. Palmer

In the opening chapter, I described my first arrival in the city of Dublin, fascinated by the orange-colored neon lights along Mount Merrion Ave. Young men from the countryside often came to the city for work. Some settled in well; others did not. For me it marked the transition into some of the most fruitful years of my life. In a very real sense Dublin became my new home. And my adult self began to grow and blossom.

Several years later, the millennial year of 2000, I landed in another city, greeted once more by neon lights. It was Manila, the capital of the Philippines. In those days they did not use a jet-bridge, so we stepped off the plane onto the tarmac. Looking at the main building, the word *Mabuhay* bounced out at me, and without any idea what the word meant I knew it was a warm greeting.

I stood on the tarmac and gazed around. It all looked so familiar. Momentarily, I doubted my own memory as I thought back on what countries I had visited, and this was certainly not one of them. As I entered the arrivals hall, I was greeted by warm smiles, by people I had never seen in my life.

Being my first time in a strange country, I had arranged to stay with a group of Irish Columban missionaries in Singalong St., Malate. But, in fact, nothing felt strange. As I walked the nearby streets, it felt as if I had known this city all my life. Nor was there any hesitation in exchanging greetings with the people who spoke to me. Filipinos are renowned for their friendly spirit, and that was my experience from the start. There was, however, also a strong sense of homoerotic attraction, the meaning of which would only emerge some years later.

Encountering Former Lives

In September 2003, I learned of an American healer who was visiting London, where I lived at the time, specializing in chakra healing. I decided to have a consultation in the hope of better understanding a recurring bowel disorder. After an initial introduction in the consulting room, the healer asked me to confirm my name and give my date of birth. She then went on to explain the process of reading my chakra field. She sat a short distance in front of me and with her eyes closed began reading my chakra energies.

After about ten minutes of silence, she began to explain that my heart chakra looked quite dark, gray, and heavy. A lot of energy concentrated there, and it needed releasing. Among the possible causes she suggested were influences from past lives (a concept I had encountered when I studied psychology but to which I never gave much attention). She informed me that she was picking up extensive information on my former lives, which she shared with me.

I was a monk in the Middle Ages heavily involved in the study of the vowed life, a topic on which I did extensive research and writing. She then opened her eyes and looking straight at me said: "And I get the impression that you have been doing similar work in this life-time." Wow! Spot on! How on earth did she know that? We had started the session as complete strangers to each other. How much more does she know about me?

She detected former lives of mine in the seventeenth and eighteenth centuries when I had a keen interest in both spirituality and science, and particularly the integration between the two, which incurred disapproval from specialists in both disciplines. That observation left me wondering how that former life impacted my current interest in science and spirituality.

Then came what can only be described as a bombshell. I had spent a number of previous lifetimes in the Philippines, during which I had several intense, complicated human relationships, many of a homosexual nature. At that stage in her disclosures, I felt like running out of the room, and she probably picked up my discomfort as her feedback moved on to how I might try to integrate all that former experience into my present life, thus lifting some of the dark cloud surrounding my heart chakra.

My initial visit to Manila and all the strange familiarity that had baffled me began to make sense. By the time the session with the healer in London occurred, I had made three visits to the Philippines and was now enmeshed in a few intense homoerotic relationships. It took another three years to deal with those intricate issues. It was intensely emotional, but, paradoxically, it drew me into deeper levels of spiritual awakening. Fortunately, back in London, I had a very skilled spiritual director who accompanied me through a difficult discernment process that often was both exhilarating and bewildering. Essentially I was undergoing yet another paschal journey.

The Expanded Self

Millions of people acknowledge that we live at a time of great change; by trusting more deeply in their adult selves, many seem to be able to ride the tides of our changing times. We seem to judge the forces of change, however, largely by external factors, be it in information technology, economic shifts, or political process. One wonders how much attention we are giving to changes coming from within. How many among us are even aware of these? And when we do become aware, how well can we articulate this evolutionary unfolding?

In chapter three above, I noted the shift from the strongly individualistic identity, promoted by Aristotle and the ancient Greeks, to the more relational one encapsulated in the phrase: "I am at all times the sum of my relationships and that is what confers my identity as a person." Despite the fact that the relational construct is widely recognized in the social sciences and among many therapists and counselors, in the public arenas of education, politics, economics, and religion, the earlier model of the robust individual reigns supreme. Meanwhile there is a rapidly evolving sense of personhood, of which connection with former lives is just one aspect.

There is a subtle but substantial shift going on here, one that is likely to become more visible and culturally accepted as we move deeper into the twenty-first century. In many ways it might turn out to be one of the more formidable paschal journeys that we will have to negotiate in the next few years. I highlight briefly three developments moving us in this new relational direction: the protean self, the cyborg, the rainbow body phenomenon.

An American psychiatrist, Robert J. Lifton, popularized the idea of the *protean self* to denote the postmodern tendency to become fluid and many-sided in our attempts to engage the flux and fluidity of our age. Named after Proteus, the Greek god of many forms, the Protean is characterized by a tendency to forgo the certainties and securities of the past, engaging instead in continuous exploration and personal experiment. Lifton contends that the postmodern self is less traumatized by modern rootlessness than we might expect, continually refashioning integrity by an ability to stay on the move between partial, incomplete, and irreconcilable realities. While this fluidity is often associated with the superficial posting of images on social media, we are dealing with an evolutionary development needing a much deeper assessment of what is at stake.

Another take on this same phenomenon, albeit with a technological rather than psychological focus, is the notion of *the cyborg*, sometimes described as the posthuman. A cyborg denotes a cybernetic organism, a person with both organic and biomechatronic body parts. The term was coined in 1960 by Manfred Clynes and Nathan S. Kline and popularized by the American feminist social scientist Donna J. Haraway. Beyond the integration of multiple personalities, as in the protean self, the central issue here is the expanded notion of self, beyond an exclusive organic identity to that of the integration of human and machine. An example that every reader will understand is that of the pacemaker, given to regulate human heart function. Let's suppose that my doctor recommends a pacemaker to regularize my heart condition, and having refused the offer, I die some months later, aged seventy-two years old. Now supposing I accept the pacemaker and live to be eighty-five. To use traditional religious language: which was God's will for me—to die at seventy-two, or live on until eighty-five? The pacemaker is not merely a piece of medical technology; it becomes an integral dimension of the life force at work in my entire being.[78]

For most of our contemporaries there is no dilemma here. To accept the pacemaker seems to be the obvious and responsible thing to do. But how many among us realize that we are fundamentally changing what it means to be human? Some fundamentalists might claim that we are playing God. It strikes me that this is an evolutionary development that God wishes us to accept and promote.

It opens up, however, a proverbial hornet's nest. According to the futurist Ray Kurzweil, by 2040, many of us will be able to go to a doctor's office and order a range of nanobite technologies (entities invisible to the human eye) that a doctor will be able to insert into our brains in order to alter one or more aspects of our behavior. I suspect this will already be happening by 2030. Might this also be God's will for us, an evolutionary advance that is ultimately for our good? Or is it the beginning of a slippery slope leading to ultimate perdition?

The great fear is this: *In whose hands will this technological power be held? And what are the ethics that will guarantee its responsible use?* How do we negotiate relevant ethical standards in a world where the traditional guardians of morality—namely, religion and the church—no longer command credibility? In several cases, they don't even understand what is evolving. Ethics and morality are now in the hands of secular powers, not necessarily governments but rather mega-corporations, for whom voracious consumption and financial superiority are the dominant values.

My third example comes from the Buddhist tradition of Asia, popularly known as the *rainbow body phenomenon.* In 1998, a Tibetan Buddhist monk named Khenpo A-Chö was able to achieve a metaphysical ancient phenomenon known as the "rainbow body." Although this was the most recent record of a rainbow body occurring, there have been over 160,000 people who have reportedly achieved a rainbow body through the Tibetan Buddhist practice of Dzogchen. Dzogchen is a collection of teachings and meditation enlightenment. Achieving a rainbow body is the result of reaching a peaked enlightened state and refers to the act of either shrinking the body before death or at the time of death. The shrinking and eventual disappearance of the physical body is understood as a complete transformation into light.[79]

From the Personal to the Transpersonal

On several fronts, what it means to be human is being stretched into new evolutionary possibilities full of promise and peril. The three examples offered above—the protean self, the cyborg, the rainbow body phenomenon—are merely the tip of a proverbial iceberg. There are also several narratives about former life experiences, largely dismissed, and even ridiculed, by modern science. Rational wisdom cannot keep up anymore. Evolution is plunging us all into greater depths of knowledge and wisdom. Mystical consciousness (as explored by the philosopher Philip Goff) is leading the way, and if we wish to survive as a species we had better come on board.

Our inherited understanding of personhood is no longer tenable or credible. It is too narrowly functional and individualistic. It needs to be re-visioned in the light of the transpersonal. That will involve a painful dying to what Herbert Marcuse one time called one-dimensional man, but it also inaugurates the launch of the transpersonal human, and therein lies a more enduring sense of hope and promise.

How we relate, individually, interpersonally, and socially, will need to be reimagined. Most formidable of all is the challenge to deal in a more informed and proactive way in the articulation of human sexuality in this new relational landscape.

Beyond Aristotelian Anthropology

For most of our time on earth, we, as a human species, operated out of a very different sense of self. In chapter four, I outlined the Aristotelian definition of the human person as the autonomous, self-reliant, separate, rational individual, which today dictates not merely our anthropology but also our education, politics, and economics. And all the major religions seem to endorse this understanding of the human person. It is a tragic and dangerous departure from the relational self that has characterized much, if not most, of our long evolutionary journey of seven million years.

As a species we are endowed with an inherited capacity for relationality and cooperation. Many among us are not even aware of that fact, and the fierce competition so endemic to our contemporary lifestyles leaves us with a deeply debilitating sense of woundedness. We need to reclaim that which is deeply inscribed in our physiological make up:

> The cells themselves are cooperative organizations. Without extensive cooperation between the molecular processes and organelles that make up cells, we would not exist. Each of our million billion cells is made up of thousands of incredibly small and intricate parts that cooperate together to produce the functions of the cell.... We are cooperators that are made of cooperators, that are made of cooperators. It is cooperation all the way down.... Wherever evolution has been able to fully exploit the benefits of cooperation, we always find the extraordinary level of specialization and interdependency that results from a high degree of division of labor. We find it within cells, within our bodies, within our social systems, and between nations. And there is every reason to believe it will also be a feature of organizations that are capable of future evolutionary success on even larger scales.[80]

The ethnological data from hunter-gatherer cultures has provided a rich resource from which to surmise how Paleolithic hunter-gatherers structured their reality, living in bands consisting of fifteen to thirty people. Among our human ancestors, the hunter-gatherer band is the oldest known human social structure. There are still hunter-gatherer bands, but precious few, and many of them are threatened with assimilation. Hundreds of examples have, however, been studied in the past century. Researchers have found that hunter-gatherers tend to live a life of economic, political, and social egalitarianism.

Central to this egalitarianism is an alternative anthropology encapsulated in this description: *I am at all times the sum of my relationships, and that is what defines my personal uniqueness.* Relationality is central not merely to who we are in the here and now but to everything happening within and around us. Today, we understand this relational capacity not merely as a human endowment but as a resourced gift we inherit from our status as Earthlings.

And beyond the earth is our cosmic identity, woven into the fabric of creation initially from the remnant of dying stars. We are stardust, and it is well beyond poetic license to claim that our destiny is written in the stars. And if we are being rebirthed in a range of lifetimes, might this not also have something to do with the death and resurrection of star energy?

Human beings are not mere organisms, defined primarily by biology and genetics. Nor are we material bodies enlivened by a God-inserted soul. More accurately, we are each a cosmic, planetary process unfolding in time and space, across many generations and several lifetimes. And each time the process unfolds into its cosmic fullness, then we yield to the transformative creativity of the Great Spirt, and our individualized energy fields return to their cosmic origins for the Spirit once more to reweave new embodied possibilities.

It is called reincarnation in some religious traditions and resurrection in others. In both cases, the envisaged outcome is largely if not solely anthropocentric (confined to the human). There is little recognition for the earthly and cosmic dimensions or for the destiny that is written in the stars. The egalitarian grandeur of our being and becoming is almost entirely suppressed. It is the personal devoid of the transpersonal, stripped of the relational empowerment that has made us the unique species we are meant to become.

Our Psychosexual Landscape

Sex in my young formative years was a dark, dangerous mystery. Even the mention of the word was prohibited. Many among us, myself included, went into our adult years not merely with suppressed emotion but more seriously with repressed psychic energy.

Repression, it seems to me, is the critical issue. Ever since Aristotle defined sexuality as a male prerogative, requiring a biological organism called a female to fertilize the male seed, we have been incarcerated in a psychic prison breeding waves of repression that have prevailed over several centuries.

For Aristotle, sex has one function only: the reproduction of the species, a biological imperative endorsed by St. Paul, Augustine, Thomas Aquinas, Martin Luther, by world religions generally, and by many governments till relatively recent times. The human capacity for intimate loving, bonding, emotional nurturing, and spiritual development, which, I suggest, are among the *primary* purposes of our sexuality, have been moralized out of existence, feeding the dark repression that has been haunting us until the mid-twentieth century.

When eventually the lid was blown off the repressed boiling cauldron in the 1960s, raw sexualized energy spewed out all over the place. It was not just the young that threw caution to the wind. The frenzied acting-out featured across a much wider age group, as it still does to the present time. Copulation became a response not so much for reproduction of the species but to express the long repressed hunger for erotic fulfillment: male and female, male and male, female and female. As we moved into the twenty-first century, the experimental climate moved further along as LGBTQI became the synonym for an ever-expanding horizon of possibilities. And as the urge for sexual release became culturally more acceptable, gender identity became the next feature in the culture of super-fluidity

Some people wonder where will it all end. I wonder whether we have even begun the process of responsible discernment—on an issue that touches the lives of every person. Despite the extensive sexual acting out and the sexual liberalism that allegedly characterizes our time, sexuality continues to be subject still couched in a great deal of toxic secrecy. Moreover, as a species we face a huge challenge of psychosexual healing, not merely for the victims of sex abuse, but for all of us who carry hurts and wounds from the centuries of repression.

This has probably been one of the most painful Calvarys that our species has had to endure, and it will take a few generations to move us toward healing and wholeness. I do detect seedlings of resurrection amid this murky background. Even within my own extended family, I see younger people, who fortunately were not trapped in sexualized guilt and shame, negotiating the new sexual landscape with a great deal more agility and wisdom. What to an older generation may seem like loose morals (for example, the extensive practice of co-habiting) is actually a proactive negotiation of a relatively new territory that in time will require a whole new psychosexual ethic.

What that ethic will look like is too soon to speculate. We don't even know who is going to create it or how it will be implemented. I cannot see the major religions making much of a contribution, stuck in a nostalgic dream to revive the monogamous heterosexuality of bygone days. Governments will need to lead the way, requiring politicians who will be sensitively aware of the complex landscape needing attention. In voting for future elected officials we will need to keep this challenge in mind.

Ours is indeed an entangled universe. Nothing makes sense in isolation anymore—if indeed it ever did. We all belong to multiple worlds and multiple selves. Technology will carry this sense of connected multiplicity to new levels wherein the integration of human and machine—what Ilia Delio calls "techno sapiens"—will elevate our interconnectedness to new levels of engagement. There are indeed major cultural and ethical challenges at stake here, but let's trust the Spirit's creative energy at the heart of our evolutionary universe.

Facing My Own Death

Ever since I studied quantum physics in the 1980s, my sense of death and afterlife changed dramatically. At the heart of this amazing universe of which we are all entangled parts, energy is the stuff that keeps us all going. And as indicated previously, I believe that all energy is energized by the Great Spirit. All energy is sacred.

It is in the erotic, birthing power of such energy that we are all born out of the world (we don't come into it—we come out of it). And in that complex formative process, initially in the creative urge of our parents, then in the fertility of our mother's womb, and finally as we arrive in the realm of space-time, field-influence sorts out how everything falls into place, in the process of birthing new life.

Much of it is obvious and can be observed and measured by humans, but the crucial dimension is hidden. It is what I referred to above as *field-influence*.[81] Around each of our bodies are a series of invisible energy fields, stretching out for approximately seventy centimeters (thirty inches). Healers work regularly with the field closest to our physical bodies, namely, the aura. Without these energy fields we cannot even exist. They ground us in the universe, connect us as Earthlings to the home planet, and sustain all the energy-based processes on which we grow and flourish from birth to death.

Experienced hospice carers often allude to their experienced sensation of energy disappearing as they sit beside a dying person. In all probability, this is the gradual disappearance of the energy fields, until nothing is left except the aura. Then that evaporates and the person will die shortly thereafter.

Here we run into the limitations of human language. Strictly speaking the energy does not disappear or evaporate. As we know from standard physics, energy is never wasted nor destroyed. Energy will always reconnect with energy and will be transformed into other embodied forms. Therefore, at my death, the energy fields that keep me alive will leave my corporeal configuration (my body) and will be integrated afresh with the great energy fields of the universe.

In this cosmic communion of saints, my evolution will continue. How, exactly, I have no idea, and, to be honest, I have not the slightest worry about all that. I trust the Great Spirit will keep me on my toes as she has done throughout my present lifetime.

And after all that? I totally endorse the wonderful declaration from Parker Palmer:

> Theologies that portray heaven as a gated community in the sky don't speak to my condition. Among other things, an eternity spent exclusively among members of my own tribe sounds more hellish than heavenly. Nor am I persuaded by claims that, when we die, spirit separates from matter and takes on some sort of disembodied wraithlike life. As far as I can tell, matter and spirit are intertwined and indivisible,

> a distinction without a difference, two sides of one coin. If flesh and earth were not infused with spirit, how could we and the natural world be so full of beauty, healing, and grace?…I am certain of two things: when we die, our bodies return to earth, and earth knows how to turn death into new life.[82]

How we will be reunited with those we have loved and cherished in this lifetime is a matter I am more than happy to leave in hands of the Great Spirit. She has maintained creation in its erotic birthing over several multiverses but also in the creative energy of every subatomic particle. She knows what she is about—let's trust her creativity!

Paradox and Synodality

> *Paradox is contradictory and unbelievable, absurd and often compelling, impossible but true. It projects the tension of opposites that are held simultaneously and is therefore given short shrift by the logical Western mind. We come up against it everywhere, and more often than not we dismiss it by saying, it's just the way it is, or it's a mystery.*
>
> —Miriam Therese Winter

After the election of Pope Leo XIV on May 8, 2025, international media frequently referenced the figure of 1.4 billion people as the current population of the Catholic Church. The figure is based on the Vatican's own statistics issued at the end of 2023, also highlighting an increase of 10 million new members in the past twenty years. Correspondingly, the total number of the ordained in the Catholic Church now stands at 407,000, a decrease of 20,000 since the year 2000. Paschal paradox looms large in the Catholic Church today. While the ranks of the faithful continue to expand, the clergy seem to be in irreversible decline.[83]

Much more disturbing for me was the media approach to the task facing the new pope. How would he try to resolve the tension between conservatives and progressives within the Catholic Church? Surely the challenge facing Pope Leo—and the Catholic people alike—is that we try to come to terms with the enormous diversity in an international family of 1.4 billion members. How do we discern the diversity at work in such a complex group? How do we honor, affirm, and celebrate such diversity? Is it even possible for any one leader, based at the heart of the old Roman Empire, to do justice to such a richly textured faith community?

The Story of Synodality

Something of that complex global entity came into focus in the final years of the papacy of Pope Francis. He convoked a synodal process inviting the Catholic people of the world into a new dialogical structure of adult conversation and egalitarian communal reconstruction. It was an exciting experiment with a range of difficult moments as trust was slowly built and divergent views on several issues were raised in a spirt of respectful dialogue. The process continues, with an unsure momentum for future progress.

With hindsight, the synodal process failed to address the clerical decline in the church today, and this omission could seriously damage its future progress. As a social scientist, I find it helpful to employ the work of the psychologist Elisabeth Kübler-Ross in assessing the synodal process.[84] Kübler-Ross famously identified five stages that occur in the grieving/dying process: denial, anger (blaming), bargaining, depression, and acceptance. We see these stages at work not merely in dying people, but also in the serious decline of organizations and institutions. In terms of the synodal process of the Catholic Church, and specifically the two major meetings held in Rome, it seems to me that *the bargaining stage* helps us to understand what was transpiring.

Although the synodal members were probably not aware of the statistics I cite above, certainly the lay participants recognized the impeding decline of clericalism, and the need to address it in a more openly discerning way. They talked around the issue rather than directly to it. They wanted to hold on to the priestly dimension, but with a great deal of ambivalence. Most of the synodal members had moved beyond the denial and anger/blaming (stages 1 and 2) and for the greater part were immersed unknowingly in stage 3. The process was—and perhaps still is—in the throes of a paschal journey with death and resurrection beckoning for more discerning attention.

The Communal Imperative

At the synodal meetings in Rome, the spiritual director appointed by Pope Francis was the Dominican theologian (now cardinal) Timothy Radcliffe, who frequently reminded the participants of the communal foundations upon which the Church grows and flourishes. Theologically, this can be traced back to the Gospel vision of the Kingdom of God, which I rename throughout this book as the Companionship of Empowerment. St Paul adopts the notion of *ecclesia* to build on that Gospel imperative. We get glimpses of this communal process at work in Acts 2:44-47 and 4:32-37, with communities gathering together, sharing all in common, and empowering new vision in line with the Gospel ideal of the new reign of God.

In 2022, a group from the controversial Jesus Seminar published a book entitled *After Jesus, Before Christianity*[85] tracing what they claim has been a long neglected element of our Christian foundations, the communal imperative. While most church historians trace the development of early Christianity—over the first 300 years—in terms of the gradual evolution of a hierarchical, institutional structure, there was a parallel movement that has been largely neglected, and perhaps even suppressed. It consisted of a range of clubs, associations, and networks, meeting frequently, exploring, debating, and advancing a communal sense of church from the ground up. And, remarkably, many of those gathering ended with sharing a meal, commonly understood to be Eucharist.

This alternative strand—documented in *After Jesus, Before Christianity*—lasted well into the fourth century, and was gradually subverted by the rise of Constantine and the institutional evolution of the Church that followed. In this context, synodality is not a new concept; rather it is the original foundation of our faith from the time of Jesus right through till the fourth century. In a sense, it was never totally suppressed, as a range of communal enterprises have arisen time and again over the 2,000 years of Christendom.

Beyond the Imperial Paradigm

As I write the Afterword for this book, I am haunted by ghastly images coming out of Gaza of emaciated children, grieving mothers, and distraught victims of a cruel war. Additionally, around our world we evidence a shift toward right-wing governments, preoccupied with protecting their own imperial power—often violently—rather than upholding and cultivating an empowering sense of community. Meanwhile, visionary and prophetic voices of our time alert us to the plight of the earth itself and the damage being done to the natural resources so necessary for a meaningful life. The communal consciousness being called forth is not merely about people, but also how to identify in a more convivial way with the Earth itself, and indeed with the entire web of life, planetary and cosmic alike.

This desire for a new global, egalitarian vision, is central to our Christian understanding of the paschal journey. The risen hope of Easter is a universal dream to which every organic creature aspires. How to translate it into action in our time remains a formidable challenge.

I sense a deep wisdom in the oft-cited admonition, "Bloom where you're planted." Might this be a fertile moment for those of us in the

Catholic faith community to bloom afresh and create an alternative vision to transcend the addictive dysfunctionality holding our world and its peoples to ransom at this time? Ilia Delio's timely reminder that catholicity is first and foremost about a communal universality springs to mind.[86]

While acknowledging the disturbing features of our church, so often highlighted by media—our clerical domination, the clerical sex scandals, our collusion with colonialism, our anti-world rhetoric, our marginalization of minority groups—there is another face to our church rarely acknowledged even by Catholics themselves. Within our universal family of 1.4 billion people (99% of whom are not clerics), compassion for the poor, liberation of the oppressed, love of the earth, educational empowerment, health-based healing, and diverse expressions of ritual and sacrament, are among our outstanding features. Our universal creativity far outweighs our systemic dysfunctionalities.

If and when the synodal process resumes, my hope and prayer is that we will face our paschal paradox in a more honest and transparent way. Priesthood as we have known it is in terminal decline, particularly in the West. Salvaging the situation by bringing in priests from the South is another example of the bargaining stage of death and dying. We are dealing with a Calvary moment which we need to embrace with vision and courage. Otherwise, clericalism will remain a resistant block to embracing the communal imperative at the heart of our faith story.

Our ecclesial resurrection will be new and different. It will be an initiative of the creative Spirit which we humans cannot engineer. In the spirit of paschal anticipation, we can ready ourselves for its arrival just as Mary Magdalene and her companions did amid the trauma and pain of their Calvary time. Like Mary in the garden, the tears will often blur our vision but our willingness to see it through and not run away will be the resurrection breakthrough for ministry in a new shape. It will be ministry serving the New Reign of God, the Companionship of Empowerment.

Awaiting our embrace and commitment is the international, multi-faceted family to which we belong, along with the internal process of becoming a community-based, empowering church once more. That must be our goal as an Easter risen people.

BIBLIOGRAPHY

Al-Khalili, Jim, and Johnjoe McFadden. *Life on the Edge*. London: Penguin/Random House, 2014.

Aslan, Raza. *God: A Human History of Religion*. London: Penguin/Corgi, 2017.

Barker, Graeme. *The Agricultural Revolution in Prehistory*. Oxford: Oxford University Press, 2009.

Bartunek, John. *Spiritual but Not Religious: The Search for Meaning in a Material World.* Charlotte, NC: Tan Books, 2019.

Beattie, Tina. *New Catholic Feminism*. New York: Routledge, 2006.

Bhabha, Homi. *The Location of Culture*. New York: Routledge, 1994.

Bidwell, Duane R. *When One Religion Isn't Enough: The Lives of Spiritually Fluid People.* Boston: Beacon Press, 2018.

Boff, Leonardo. *Ecology and Liberation*. Maryknoll, NY: Orbis Books, 1995.

———. *Come Holy Spirit*. Maryknoll, NY: Orbis, 2015.

Boros, Ladislaus. *Meeting God in Man*. London: Search Press, 1968.

———. *The Mystery of Death*. New York: Herder & Herder, 1965.

———. *Pain and Providence*. London: Search Press, 1966.

Bregman, Rutger. *Humankind: A Hopeful History*. New York: Bloomsbury Publishing, 2020.

Brock, Rita N., and Rebecca Parker. *Saving Paradise*. Boston: Beacon Press, 2008.

Brueggemann, Walter. *The Book That Breathes New Life*. Minneapolis: Augsburg Fortress, 2005.

———. *The Hopeful Imagination*. Minneapolis: Fortress, 1986.

———. *Reality, Grief, Hope: Three Urgent Prophetic Tasks*. Grand Rapids, MI: Eerdmans, 2014.

Cannato. Judy. *Radical Amazement*. Notre Dame, IN: Sorin Books, 2006.

Capra, Fritjof. "Complexity and Life." *Theory, Culture and Society* 22, no. 1 (2005): 33–44.

Caputo, John D. *Hoping against Hope*. Minneapolis: Fortress, 2015.

Clooney, Francis Xavier. *Comparative Theology.* London: Wiley-Blackwell, 2010.

Clough, David. *On Animals: Systematic Theology.* London: Bloomsbury, 2013.

———. *On Animals: Theological Ethics.* London: Bloomsbury, 2018.

Clynes, Manfred, and Nathan Klein. "Cyborgs and Space." *Astronautics* 14 (1960): 26–27.

Cook-Greuter, Susan. *Transcendence and Mature Thought in Adulthood.* Lanham, MD: Rowman and Littlefield, 1994.

Cornille, Catherine. "Introduction: The Dynamics of Multiple Belonging." In *Many Mansions? Multiple Religious Belonging and Christian Identity*, edited by

Catherine Cornille. Maryknoll, NY: Orbis Books, 2010.
Crossan, John Dominic. *The Historical Jesus.* San Francisco: HarperSanFrancisco, 1991.
———. *Who Is Jesus?* New York: HarperCollins, 1996.
Crossan, John Dominic, and Sarah Sexton. *Resurrecting Easter.* New York: HarperOne, 2018.
Crosby, Michael. *Repair My House!* Maryknoll, NY: Orbis Books, 2012.
Currivan, Jude. *The Cosmic Hologram.* Rochester, VT: Inner Traditions, 2017.
Dean-Drummond, Celia. *Creaturely Theology: on God, Humans and Other Animals,* 2009.
Deane-Drummond, Celia, Sigurd Bergmann, and Markus Vogt, eds. *Religion in the Anthropocene.* Eugene, OR: Cascade Books, 2017.
de Chardin, Teilhard. *The Divine Milieu.* London: Collins/Fontana, 1961.
———. *Hymn of the Universe.* London: Collins/Fontana, 1960.
———. *The Phenomenon of Man.* London: Collins/Fontana, 1959.
Delio, Ilia. *Birth of a Dancing Star.* Maryknoll, NY: Orbis Books, 2019.
______. *Christ in Evolution.* Maryknoll, NY: Orbis Books, 2008.
______. *Making All Things New.* Maryknoll, NY: Orbis Books, 2015.
______. *The Unbearable Wholeness of Being.* Maryknoll, NY: Orbis Books, 2013.
Dunn, James G. D. *Unity and Diversity in the New Testament.* London: SCM Press, 1976.
Eagleton, Terry. *On Evil.* New Haven, CT: Yale University Press, 2010.
Ehrman, Bart. *The Triumph of Christianity.* London: Oneworld, 2018.
Eisenstein, Charles. *Sacred Economics.* Berkeley, CA: Evolver Editions, 2011.
Fox, Matthew. *Original Blessing.* Santa Fe, NM: Bear, 1983.
Fowler, James. *Stages of Faith.* San Francisco: Harper & Row, 1981.
Fuentes, Agustin. *The Creative Spark.* New York: Dutton, 2017.
Goff, Philip. *Galileo's Error: Foundations for a New Science of Consciousness.* New York: Pantheon Books, 2019.
Haight, Roger. *Faith and Evolution.* Maryknoll, NY: Orbis Books, 2019.
Haraway, Donna J. "Manifesto for Cyborgs: Science, Technology, and Socialist Feminism in the 1980s." *Socialist Review,* 80 (1985): 65–108.
———. *The Companion Species Manifesto: Dogs, People, and Significant Otherness.* Chicago: Prickly Paradigm Press, 2003.
———. *When Species Meet.* Minneapolis: University of Minnesota Press, 2008.
Haught, John F. *Making Sense of Evolution.* Louisville, KY: Westminster John Knox Press, 2010.
———. *Resting on the Future.* New York: Bloomsbury, 2015.
Hawken, Paul. *Blessed Unrest.* New York: Viking, 2007.
Hedges, Paul. "Multiple Religious Belonging after Religion." *Open Theology* 3 (2017): 48–72.

Heffner, Philip. *The Human Factor*. Minneapolis: Fortress, 1993.
Heinrich, Bernd. *Life Everlasting: The Animal Way of Death*. New York: Mariner Books, 2013.
Hill, Jason. *Becoming a Cosmopolitan*. Lanham, MD: Rowman & Littlefield, 2000.
Horan, Daniel P. *Catholicity and Emerging Personhood*. Maryknoll, NY: Orbis Books, 2019.
Hostie, Raymond. *Vie et Mort des Ordres Religieux*. Paris: Desclee de Brower, 1972.
Howard-Brook, Wes. *"Come Out My People!"* Maryknoll, NY: Orbis Books, 2011.
———. *Empire Baptized*. Maryknoll, NY: Orbis Books, 2016.
Jensen, Robin. *The Cross: History, Art, and Controversy*, Cambridge, MA: Harvard University Press, 2017.
Johnson, Elizabeth. *Ask the Beasts*. New York: Bloomsbury, 2014.
———. *Creation and the Cross*. Maryknoll, NY: Orbis Books, 2018.
———. *Quest for the Living God*. New York: Continuum, 2006.
Johnson, Kurt, and David R. Ord. *The Coming Inter-Spiritual Age*. Vancouver: Namaste Publishing, 2012.
Kaku, Michio. *Physics of the Impossible*. New York: Doubleday, 1999.
Keller, Catherine. *Face of the Deep*. New York: Routledge, 2003.
Kelly, Anthony J. "Human Consciousness, God and Creation." *Pacifica: Australasian Theological Studies* 28 (2005): 3–22.
Kendig, H., et al. "Thirty Years of the United Nations and Global Ageing: An Australian Perspective." *Australasian Journal on Ageing* 32, supp. 2 (2013): 28–34.
King, Karen L. *The Gospel of Mary of Magdala: Jesus and the First Woman Apostle*. Santa Rosa, CA: Polebridge Press, 2003.
Kubler-Ross, Elisabeth. *On Death and Dying*. New York: Methuen, 1969.
Kurzweil, Ray. *The Singularity Is Near*. New York: Viking, 2005.
Kyung, Chung Hyun. *Struggle to Be the Sun Again*. Maryknoll, NY: Orbis Books, 1990.
Lanzetta, Beverly. *The Monk Within*. Sebastopol, CA: Blue Sapphire Books, 2018.
Latham, Katherine J. "Human Health and the Neolithic Revolution: An Overview of Impacts of the Agricultural Transition on Oral Health, Epidemiology, and the Human Body." *Nebraska Anthropologist* 187. http://digitalcommons.unl.edu/nebanthro/187.
Lee, Hyo-Dong. *Spirit, Qi, and the Multitude*. New York: Fordham University Press, 2014.
———. "My Path to a Theology of Qi." In *Theology without Walls*, edited by Jerry L. Martin, 234–42. New York: Routledge, 2020.
Levy, Paul. *The Quantum Revelation*. New York: Select Books, 2018.
Lifton, Robert. *The Protean Self*. New York: Basic Books, 1993.

Lovelock, James. *Gaia: A New Look at Life on Earth*. New York: Oxford University Press, 1979.
MacKenzie, Catriona, and Natalie Stoljar. *Relational Autonomy*. New York: Oxford University Press, 2000.
Martin, Jerry L., ed. *Theology without Walls*. New York: Routledge, 2019.
McGowan, Annie. *Eucharistic Epicleses, Ancient and Modern*. London: SPCK, 2014.
Mitchell, Stephen, and Peter van Nuffelen. *One God: Pagan Monotheism in the Roman Empire*. Cambridge: Cambridge University Press, 2010.
Moore, Stephen D. *Divinanimality: Animal Theory, Creaturely Theology*. New York: Fordham University Press, 2014.
Moss, Candida. *The Myth of Persecution*. New York: Harper/Collins, 2014.
Nolan, Albert. *Jesus before Christianity*. London: Darton, Longman & Todd, 1977.
Oliver, Tom. *The Self Delusion*. London: Weidenfeld & Nicolson, 2020.
O'Connell, Maureen, Compassion: *Loving our Neighbours in an Age of Globalization*, Maryknoll, NY: Orbis Books, 2009.
O'Loughlin, Thomas. *The Eucharist*. New York: Bloomsbury, 2015.
O'Murchu, Diarmuid. *Adult Faith*. Maryknoll, NY: Orbis Books, 2010.
———. *Ancestral Grace*. Maryknoll, NY: Orbis Books, 2012.
———. *Beyond Original Sin*. Maryknoll, NY: Orbis Books, 2018.
———. *Christianity's Dangerous Memory*. New York: Crossroad, 2011
———. *Doing Theology in an Evolutionary Way*. Maryknoll, NY: Orbis Books, 2021.
———. *Incarnation: A New Evolutionary Threshold*. Maryknoll, NY: Orbis Books, 2017.
———. *Inclusivity: A Gospel Mandate*. Maryknoll, NY: Orbis Books, 2015.
———. *In the Beginning Was the Spirit*. Maryknoll, NY: Orbis Books, 2011.
———. *On Being a Postcolonial Christian*. North Charleston, SC: CreateSpace, 2014.
Oostveen, Daan F. "Multiple Religious Belonging and the 'Deconstruction' of Religion." *Exchange* 47, no. 1 (YEAR): 39–52.
Palmer, Parker J. *Gravity and Grace: On the Brink of Everything*. Oakland, CA: Berrett-Koehler, 2019.
Patterson, Stephen J. *Beyond the Passion*. Minneapolis: Augsburg Fortress, 2004.
———. *The Lost Way*. New York: HarperOne, 2014.
Pigliucci, Massimo, and Gerd B. Muller, eds. *Evolution: The Extended Synthesis*. Cambridge, MA: The MIT Press, 2010.
Pitre, Brant. *Jesus and the Jewish Roots of Eucharist*. New York: Random House, 2011.
Plotkin, Bill. *Nature and the Human Soul*. Novata, CA: New World Library, 2008.

Primark, Joel, and Nancy Abrams. *The View from the Center of the Universe*. New York: Riverhead Books, 2007.

Pugh, Ben. *Atonement Theories*. Eugene, OR: Wipf & Stock, 2015.

Quammen, David. *Spillover: Animal Infections and the Next Human Pandemic*. New York: W. W. Norton & Co., 2012.

Rambo, Shelly. *Spirit and Trauma*. Louisville, KY: Westminster John Knox Press, 2010.

Rawls, John. *Justice as Fairness*. Cambridge, MA: Harvard University Press, 1985.

———. *A Theory of Justice*. Cambridge, MA: Harvard University Press, 1971.

Ray, Kathleen Darby. *Deceiving the Devil: Atonement, Abuse, and Ransom*. Cleveland, OH: Pilgrim Press, 1998.

Raymo, Chet. *When God Is Gone, Everything Is Holy*. Notre Dame, IN: Sorin Books, 2008.

Reid-Bowen, Paul. *Goddess as Nature*. Farnham, UK: Ashgate, 2007.

Rilke, Rainer Maria. *Letters to a Young Poet*. New York: W.W. Norton & Co., 1993.

Robinette, Brian D. "The Difference Nothing Makes: *Creatio ex Nihilo*, Resurrection, and Divine Gravity." *Theological Studies* 72, no. 3 (YEAR): 525–57.

Rohr, Richard. *The Universal Christ*. New York: Convergent, 2019.

Rolheiser, Ron. *The Holy Longing: The Search for a Christian Spirituality*. New York: Doubleday, 1999.

Roszak, Theodore. *The Longevity Revolution*. Berkeley, CA: Berkeley Hill Books, 2001.

———. *The Making of an Elder Culture*. Gabriola Island, BC: New Society Publishers, 2009.

Rowland, Christopher. "Living with Idols: An Exercise in Biblical Theology." In *Idolatry*, edited by Stephen Barton, 163–76. London: T. & T. Clark, 1998.

Ruether, Rosemary Radford. *Women and Redemption*. London: SCM Press, 1998.

Schafer, Lothar. *Infinite Potential: What Quantum Physics Reveals*. New York: Random House, 2013.

Sheehan, Thomas. *The First Coming*. New York: Random House, 1986.

Sheldrake, Rupert. *The Presence of the Past*. New York: Times Books, 1988.

Sinclair, David, and Matthew D. LaPlante. *Lifespan: Why We Age, and Why We Don't Have To*. London: HarperCollins, 2019.

Soelle, Dorothee. *The Silent Cry*. Minneapolis: Fortress Press, 1999.

Sorokim, Pitrim. *Modern Historical and Social Philosophies*. New York: Dover Publications, 1950.

Spitzer, Michael. *The Musical Human*. New York: Bloomsbury, 2021.

Spong, John Shelby. *Biblical Literalism: A Gentile Heresy*. New York: HarperOne, 2016.

———. *The Fourth Gospel: Tales of a Jewish Mystic.* New York: HarperOne, 2013.
———. *Jesus for the Non-Religious.* San Francisco: HarperCollins, 2007.
Stanley, Christopher, ed. *The Colonized Apostle,* Minneapolis: Fortress Press, 2011.
Stewart, John. *Evolution's Arrow.* Canberra: Chapman Press, 2000.
Swimme, Brian, and Thomas Berry. *The Universe Story.* New York: Penguin, 1992.
Swimme, Brian, and Mary Evelyn Tucker. *Journey of the Universe.* New Haven, CT: Yale University Press, 2011.
Tarnas, Richard. *Cosmos and Psyche.* New York: Viking, 2006.
Taussig, Hal. *In the Beginning Was the Meal.* Minneapolis: Fortress, 2009.
Varkey, Mothy. *Church and Diakonia in the Age of Covid 19.* Delhi: ISPCK, 2020.
Vearncombe, Erin, Bernard Brandon Scott, Hal Tausig, and Sue Monk Kidd. *After Jesus, Before Christianity.* New York: HarperOne, 2022.
von Betalanffy, Ludwig. *Problems of Life.* New York: Harper, 1952. (Reprinted in 2014 by Martino Fine Books.)
Waldrop, M. *Complexity: The Emerging Science at the Edge of Order.* New York: Simon & Schuster, 1992.
Weatherall, James Owen. *Void: The Strange Physics of Nothing.* New Haven, CT: Yale University Press, 2017.
Winter, Miriam Therese. *Paradoxology: Spirituality in a Quantum Universe.* Maryknoll, NY: Orbis Books, 2009.
Wirzba, Norman. *Food and Faith: A Theology of Eating.* New York: Cambridge University Press, 2011.
Wittberg, Patricia. *The Rise and Fall of Catholic Religious Orders.* Albany: State University of New York Press, 1994.
Yong, Ed. *I Contain Multitudes.* London: Vintage, 2016.

Chapter One: My Evolutionary Horizon

1. For the Eastern Orthodox Church, the world began in 5508 BCE; the early Syrian Christians put it at 5490 BCE. After careful mathematical calculation, the seventeenth-century bishop of Ussher (UK) claimed that the world began in 4004 BCE. The Hebrew Bible, for several contemporary evangelical groups, situates it around 3700 BCE.

2. Throughout much of the nineteenth century, the research focused on Neanderthal man (the eponymous skeleton was found in 1856, but there had been finds elsewhere since 1830). The idea that humans are similar to certain great apes had been obvious to people for some time, but the idea of the biological evolution of species in general was not legitimized until after Charles Darwin published *On the Origin of Species* in 1859.

3. To this date also, we can now trace the creative origins of ancient stone work, "We are first and foremost," writes the anthropologist Augustin Fuentes, "a species singularly distinguished and shaped by creativity... (We) had acquired abilities enabling novel creative behaviour by 4.4. million years ago." (Fuentes 2017, 2; 29). The Dutch historian Rutger Bregman makes an equally compelling case in his inspiring book, *Humankind* (Bregman 2020). I offer some tentative religious and theological implications in a number of books, especially, O'Murchu 2008, 2017, 2018.

4. For example, at the level of microbiology, the process includes destructive outcomes such as parasitism in which the parasite benefits while the host is harmed. Mutualism is the term used when both organisms benefit from the relationship. (More in Yong 2016).

5. Ilia Delio, *Birth of a Dancing Star*, 189, 210.

6. Much of the exploration was initially inspired by a contribution from the French philosopher Jacques Derrida, "The animal therefore I am" (a riposte to Descartes: "I think, therefore I am"), published in French in 1999 and in English in 2002, two years before Derrida's death in 2004.

7. For a valuable and informed scientific basis for this claim, see Tom Oliver, *The Self Delusion*.

8. An example that springs to mind is the development of ecopsychology in the 1990s. Theodore Roszak is credited with coining the term "ecopsychology" in his 1992 book, *The Voice of the Earth*, although a group of psychologists and environmentalists in Berkeley, including Mary Gomes and Allen Kanner, were independently using the term to describe their own work at the same time. Roszak,

Gomes, and Kanner later expanded the idea in the 1995 anthology *Ecopsychology.* Two other books were especially formative for the field, Paul Shepard's 1982 volume, *Nature and Madness*, which explored the effect that our ever-diminishing engagement with wild nature has on human psychological development, and philosopher David Abram's *The Spell of the Sensuous: Perception and Language in a More-than-Human World,* published in 1996.

9. Delio, *Birth of a Dancing Star*, i.

10. As a basic working definition of the paschal journey, I adopt this brief outline from the religious writer Ron Rolheiser (*Holy Longing*, 147): "The paschal mystery…is a process of transformation within which we are given both new life and new spirit. It begins with suffering and death, moves on to the reception of new life, spends some time grieving the old and adjusting to the new, and finally, only after the old life has been truly let go of, is a new spirit given for the life we are already living."

Chapter Two: In the Shadow of Religious Fear

11. Write into your Google search "Knowing your Bioregion," and several options will surface.

12. Of particular significance were the following books, *Pain and Providence* (Boros, 1966) and *Meeting God in Man* (Boros, 1968).

13. The first books of Teilhard that I read were *The Divine Milieu, Hymn of the Universe*, and *The Phenomenon of Man.*

14. Defined in Jungian psychology to describe the temporally coincident occurrences of acausal events. Jung spoke of synchronicity as being an "acausal connecting principle" (i.e., a pattern of connection that is not explained by causality).

15. I borrow this description from the pacifist mystical writer Evelyn Underhill (d.1941) who, in her book *The Spiritual Life* (1936, 61) describes the spiritual life as a willed correspondence of the little human spirit with the infinite Spirit

16. Two books that honor and contextualize the more adult approach to the God question are *The Case for God* (Karen Armstrong, 2010) and *God: A Human History* (Reza Aslan, 2018).

17. The three paradigms are outlined in greater detail in a previous work (O'Murchu, 2021). Another valuable resource for this expanded analysis is Jerry Martin's *Theology without Walls* (2019).

18. From Walter Brueggemann, *The Book That Breathes New Life*, 9. *Obedience* may seem a strange word here, but keep in mind the Latin origin, *obaudiere,* which means to listen attentively.

Chapter Three: Engaging the Paschal Journey of Religious Life

19. A valuable endorsement of Hostie's approach is provided by Sr. Patricia Wittberg (1994), incorporating additional wisdom and insight from extensive sociological research.

20. These are a mere handful of the leading scholarly sources: Rudolf Bultmann, *The Coming of the Kingdom of God* (1926); Norman Perrin, *The Kingdom of God in the Teaching of Jesus* (1963); Wendell Lee Willis, *The Kingdom of God in Twentieth-Century* Interpretation (1987); John P. Meier, *A Marginal Jew*, vol. 2 (1994); John Fuellenbach, *The Kingdom of God* (1995)

21. For well over fifty years now, theologians and scripture scholars have been searching for an alternative wording for *the Kingdom of God* in a desire to get away from the patriarchal imperial connotation which they claim Jesus strongly resisted. Among the alternatives suggested are: New Reign of God, *Basileia* (Greek word for *kingdom*), Realm of God, Kindom, Household of God. Originally, I borrowed the phrase *Companionship of Empowerment* from the scripture scholar John Dominic Crossan (1991, 421-422) because it seems to reflect more accurately the original Aramaic in which Jesus would have spoken. Empowerment clearly denotes sharing or giving away one's power, and the awkward word *companionship* denotes a whole new way of mediating power through communal process (as in Basic Ecclesial Communities). For more detailed explanation, see O'Murchu 2011a; 2017; 2021.

22. We need to note in passing that Trinitarian theology, over recent decades, has been moving in the same direction. See the valuable overview in Johnson (2006).

23. Almost single-handedly, the American scholar Wes Howard Brook (2016) grounds the New Testament understanding of the kingdom of God in the original creation story of Genesis 1.

24. *Autonomy* is probably the most frequently cited characteristic in the contemporary understanding of the human person. Those who promote a culture of human rights, frequently underestimating (or ignoring) responsibilities and duties, strongly emphasize human autonomy, above and beyond other life forms. MacKenzie and Stoljar (2000) provide a comprehensive and well-thought-through analysis of this phenomenon, highlighting that the only autonomy that will serve humanity well (along with other creatures) is a relational rather than adversarial one.

25. This emphasis on rationality is not merely a human endowment. For Aristotle it is a divine quality: "The human being is the only erect animal because its nature and essence is divine; the function of the most divine is thinking and being intelligent" (*De partibus animalium* 4.10.686a.27–29). In both the *Nichomachean Ethics* and in *De Anima* 3, Aristotle writes extensively about human flourishing

and the happiness (*eudaimonia*) that ensues. Indeed, he views the human as made in the image of God (*imago Dei*)—very impressive at first sight, and heavily endorsed by philosophers over the past two millennia. For a contemporary analysis of the notion of *imago Dei* in scripture and theology, I highly recommend the comprehensive overview of the Franciscan scholar Daniel P. Horan (2019).

26. Rohr, *Universal Christ*, 15, 18, 163.

27. Brueggemann, *Reality, Grief, Hope*, 83.

Chapter Four: Dealing with the Sting of Death

28. Aslan, *God*, 9.

29. Philosopher-turned-economist Charles Eisenstein (2011) makes the astute observation that our capitalistic money system is a notable exception to this universal process of birth and death. While everything else in creation wears out and dies, we don't allow this to happen to our money system. Our money has been given an immortal value—similar, indeed, to a God we worship. Eisenstein claims that we would have a far more dynamic and empowering economic system if we allowed our money to occasionally lose its value, decay, and become redundant.

30. Kaku, *Physics of the Impossible*, 172.

31. Eagleton, *On Evil*, 101.

32. Eagleton, *On Evil*, 143.

33. Crossan, *Who Is Jesus?*, 79.

34. Most Christian readers will assume that I am referring to the male apostles (the twelve), but in fact those I have primarily in mind are the women disciples referred to in the resurrection scene in all four Gospels. As I indicate in a previous work (O'Murchu, 2015), I believe these were the original disciples who laid the foundations of the Christian church, but our patriarchal, misogynist history has virtually obliterated their foundational witness to the building up of the earliest Christian communities. More on this topic in chapter five below.

Chapter Five: Beyond Patriarchal Insularism

35. For background evidence for these claims, I refer the reader to two sources that are well researched and accessible to the general reader, Reza Aslan's *God: A Human History of Religion* and Bart Ehrman, *The Triumph of Christianity*.

36. For the possible sources, and interpretations of this third-century, Apollo-based oracle, probably used in a ritual context, see Angelos Chaniotis in Mitchell and van Nuffelen, *One God*, 116. Equating God with the Aether (ether) should not be quickly dismissed, since the renowned scientist Albert Einstein declared it to be an unnecessary hypothesis. In the Greek cosmogonies, Aether was

considered as one of the elementary substances out of which the universe was formed. Mythologically, Aether is the god of the upper air, the purest, finest air that the gods breathe. At the time, it was thought that in order for light to travel through a vacuum, there must have been a medium filling the void through which it could propagate, as sound goes through air or ripples in a pool. This was a hotly debated scientific issue in the seventeeth and eighteenth centuries, and Christiaan Huygens proposed the notion of luminiferous aether in which light traveled in the form of longitudinal waves via an "omnipresent, perfectly elastic medium having zero density, called aether." Despite the fact that Albert Einstein found an alternative explanation in his theory of general relativity, the concept can fruitfully be employed in the understanding of energy and vacuum states in quantum physics. And the supplementary question engaging the theologian is this: What energizes the energy that underpins everything in creation? The notion of the Great Spirit is likely to be as authentic a response as we can hope for.

37. Chung Hyun Kyung, *Struggle to Be the Sun Again*, 73-74.

38. We know very little about Mary Magdalene, but the past forty years have witnessed some painstaking efforts to piece together a credible account of her central role, not merely in the life and ministry of the historical Jesus, but in the apostolic trust of the early church as well. Karen King, professor of divinity at Harvard University, is generally recognized as a leading authority on Mary Magdalene and the Gospel of Mary (King, 2003). Other influential works include Jane Schaberg, *The Death and Resurrection of Mary Magdalene* (2002); Ann Graham Brock, *Mary Magdalene: The First Apostle* (2003); Cynthia Bourgeault, *The Meaning of Mary Magdalene* (2010).

39. Brueggemann, *The Hopeful Imagination*, 9, 43, 44.

40. Some scholars suggest that Mary Magdalene herself might be the beloved disciple uniquely referenced in John's Gospel. See Esther A. de Boer, *The Gospel of Mary: Beyond a Gnostic and a Biblical Mary Magdalene* (2004); Robin Griffith-Jones, *Beloved Disciple: The Misunderstood Legacy of Mary Magdalene, the Woman Closest to Jesus* (2008); Ivonne Montijo, *Mary Magdalene: Beloved Wife, Beloved Disciple* (2017).

Chapter Six: Entangled with the Earth

41. I am trying to keep matters as simple as possible for the average reader. On their own, these statistics make little scientific sense. They are all features of the process known as photosynthesis. The statistics are helpful, however, to get the counterintuitive message that the tree draws relatively little from its roots in terms of attaining its fuller potential. One time at a conference in Nairobi, Kenya, I offered these statistics culminating with the remark that 90 percent of the growth

of a tree comes from outside the tree. A gentleman in the audience raised his hand, introduced himself as a professor of botany at an American university and went on to challenge my cited figure of 90 percent stating: "When we teach botany these days we tell the students that the roots contribute a mere 2 percent to the growth and development of tree." I was 8 percent off!

42. And beyond its scientific significance, we note some theological correlates as outlined by the Canadian eco-theologian Matthew Eaton (in Deal-Drummond, et al., 2017, 202ff.)

43. On creativity as a primary divine characteristic, see Gordan Kaufman (2004). For a comprehensive treatment of human creativity, going back into deep time, see Agustin Fuentes (2017) and Michael Spitzer (2021).

44. See Boff, *Come Holy Spirit*, 2015.

45. Caputo, *Hoping against Hope*, 179, 198.

46. This has nothing to do with pantheism (which literally means God confined to the material creation), nor is panentheism (God in all things) particularly helpful to grasp what is at stake. We are dealing with a spirit-Spirit interconnectedness, mediated primarily through the Earth, that transcends our inherited philosophical understandings of both immanence and transcendence.

47. There are several substantial theological issues here that I have briefly reviewed in previous works and will not elaborate on here. For the relevant information, see O'Murchu, *In the Beginning Was the Spirit*, 2011.

48. Therefore, the creating role traditionally attributed to the Father (*ex nihilo*) might better be renamed as a birthing energy. And the metaphor of birthing more appropriately belongs to a female than to the dominant male, which indeed might be one of the reasons for the ancient belief in God as the Great Earth Goddess (more in Reid-Bowen, 2007).

49. In which case, Mary's unique female embodiment is also undermined. For more, see Elizabeth Johnson (2003).

50. With Mary, the mother of Jesus and other women, according to Acts 1:12ff., but when it comes to Acts 2:1–4, it is only the reconstituted group of the twelve apostles. There is no reference to a female being present. The popular imagery of Mary in the midst of the twelve belongs to early Christian art, not to the text of Acts 2, the one used across all Christian churches on Pentecost Sunday.

51. Cited in Stanley, 2011, 206.

Chapter Seven: The Death and Resurrection of Liberation

52. The critics usually fail to cite the rest of the same passage in which Marx speaks of religion as the heart of a heartless world (cf. Caputo, 2016, 58).

53. Sacrificial animal offerings have featured in several ancient religious practices;

it is difficult to date the origin or development of such practices. W. Robertson Smith (in *The Religion of the Semites*, 2nd ed. [London: Black, 1907]), for example, traced the origins of sacrifice to a community's consumption of the totem animal in a festival meal, evidence for which cannot be reliably dated beyond 5000 BCE. He considered other kinds of sacrifice, including human sacrifice, to be corrupted forms of this original communion meal. Many other theorists have also emphasized the primacy of animal offerings, though in diverse ways. Thus Edward Tylor's gift theory of sacrifice defined the offering of humans as a version of cannibalism, that is, as an alternative food offering to animal meat. Henri Hubert and Marcel Mauss based their sociological theory on the most complete descriptions of sacrificial rituals available to them, the animal offerings of the Vedic (Indian) and biblical (Jewish) traditions. Walter Burkert traced sacrifice back to the hunting of animals, Jonathan Z. Smith to the domestication of animals, and Marcel Detienne to the cooking of animal meat. Barbara Ehrenreich, combining elements drawn from Burkert and Bloch, suggested that the primordial experience of being hunted by large predators conditioned humans to accept the deaths of individuals for the sake of the larger community, a precarious condition ritualized both in sacrifice and in war. James G. Frazer collated a wide variety of rituals into a theory of sacrificial kingship in which the ritual sacrifice of kings undergirds most forms of traditional ritual, including the occasional sacrifice of human beings. Maurice Bloch argued that "rebounding violence" underlies not just sacrifices, but almost all religious and political rituals and leads to the symbolic or actual domination of others through violence.

54. Spong, *Biblical Literalism*, 206ff.

55. Johnson, *Creation and the Cross*, 189.

56. Brock and Parker, *Saving Paradise*, ix.

57. Jensen, *The Cross*, 15;179.

58. Brock and Parker, *Saving Paradise*, xiv. As far as we know, the word *paradise* was coined by Xenophon, in the fifth century BCE to describe the perfection of a Persian garden.

59. This interpretation of martyrdom in early Christian times is congruent with the comprehensive critique of church historian Candida Moss, who writes: "The view of the Church as continually and unrelentingly persecuted throughout history is a myth, a myth that was solidified after the conversion of the emperor, Constantine, for purposes of retelling the history of Christianity, supporting the authority of Bishops, financing religious buildings, and marginalizing the view of heretics....In spinning this grand narrative of persecution, we forget to look for the causes of violence, and we buy into a polarized view of the world in which our opponents are evil" (Moss, *The Myth of Persecution*, 256, 258).

60. Crossan and Crossan, *Resurrecting Easter*, 9, 22.
61. Some earlier attempts include works such as Kathleen Darby Ray (1998), Rosemary Radford Ruether (1998), Stephen J. Patterson (2004).
62. South African theologian Albert Nolan captures well the mood of the time when he writes: "It would have been impossible for the people of Jesus' time to have thought of him as an eminently religious man who steered clear of political action. They would have seen him as a blasphemously irreligious man who under the cloak of religion was undermining all the values upon which religion, politics, economics, and society were based. He was a dangerous and subtly subversive revolutionary" (Nolan, *Jesus before Christianity*, 122).
63. In his commentary on John's Gospel John Shelby Spong writes: "Nowhere does John give credibility to the dreadful, guilt-producing and guilt-filled mantra that 'Jesus dies for our sins.' There is rather an incredible new insight into the meaning of life. We are not fallen; we are simply incomplete. We do not need to be rescued, but to experience the power of an all-embracing love. Our call is not to be forgiven, or even to be redeemed; it is to step beyond our limits into a new understanding of what it means to be human. John's rendition of Jesus' message is that the essence of life is discovered when one is free to give life away, that love is known in the act of loving and that the call of human life is to be all that each of us can be and then to be an agent of empowering others to be all that they can be" (Spong, *The Fourth Gospel*, 206).
64. Johnson, *Creation and the Cross*, 224, 225.
65. Johnson, *Creation and the Cross*, 185.

Chapter Eight: When the Able-bodied Ruled the World

66. Palmer, *Gravity and Grace*, 2, 8.
67. James Fowler moved from consideration of mid-lifers straight into his treatment of the elderly, the universalizing stage, which he postulated for anybody from forty-five years onward, a development attained by the rare few. Other researchers, notably, Susanne Cook-Greuter (1994), Bill Plotkin (2008), and Kenneth Stokes (1982), provide a more refined analysis of this final stage. Plotkin divides it into two stages (early and late elderhood), as I do in my own research (see O'Murchu, 2010).
68. Boff, *Ecology and Liberation*, 161–62, 70.
69. Soelle, *The Silent Cry*, 253.

Chapter Nine: The Death and Resurrection of Catholicism

70. The originality I allude to is based on a discerning analysis of *all* the meals Jesus shared with his followers, not merely one meal, namely, the last supper, which in

this context is better understood as a friendship meal and not a Passover, which followed a pattern of selective participation as indicated by Brian Pitre (*Jesus and the Jewish Roots of Eucharist*, 56–57): Passover was an act of thanksgiving for deliverance from death. It was not an open table but a covenant meal. Only Israelites could eat of it. Participants had be circumcised and recognized members of Israel. In other words, it was no ordinary meal but an exclusive family ritual—for God's chosen people. Eucharistic scholars such as Hal Taussig (2009), Norman Wirzba (2011), Annie McGowan (2014), and Thomas O'Loughlin (2015) highlight both the Calvary and resurrection of our eucharistic paschal journey.

71. The American author James Carroll captures the religious imperialism that ensued when he writes: "But under Emperor Constantine, in the fourth century, Christianity effectively became the imperial religion and took on the trappings of the empire itself. A diocese was originally a Roman administrative unit. A basilica, a monumental hall where the emperor sat in majesty, became a place of worship. A diverse and decentralized group of churches was transformed into a quasi-imperial institution—centralized and hierarchical, with the bishop of Rome reigning as a monarch. Church councils defined a single set of beliefs as orthodox, and everything else as heresy" (*The Atlantic*, June 2019).

72. Here we need to note an important distinction between *priesthood* and clericalism. From early Christian times, priesthood was understood as the *servus servorum Dei* (servant of the servants of God) with service as an unambiguous priority. Clericalism is about power and therefore marks a significant departure from the notion of priestly service. Contemporary Christianity, and particularly Catholicism, cannot hope to resolve several issues of abuse until this distinction is reinvoked.

73. Named after a Dutch theologian, Cornelius Jansen (d. 1638), Jansenism was a distinct movement within the Catholic Church, which flourished mainly in France in the seventeenth and eighteenth centuries. It strongly emphasized original sin, human depravity, the necessity of divine grace, and predestination. Although explicitly condemned by Pope Innocent X in 1653 and Pope Clement XI in 1713, it was endorsed and supported by several Catholic leaders at the time and also influenced other Christian denominations.

74. . James A. Brundage and Elizabeth M. Makowski, "Enclosure of nuns: the decretal *Periculoso* and its commentators," *Journal of Medieval History*, 20:2, June 1994, 143-155.

75. Beattie, *New Catholic Feminism*, 223.

76. The evolving shape of this synthesis, even the language we use, will be significantly different as I outline in another work (O'Murchu, 2021)

77. Raymo, *When God Is Gone, Everything Is Holy*, 112, 119.

Chapter Ten: Holding Integrity in a Liminal Impasse

78. For a more extensive overview, one that is very readable but scientifically rigorous, see Delio, *Birth of a Dancing Star*, 179–93.

79. See the brief description by Professor Michael Sheehy, University of Virginia (https://www.lionsroar.com/what-is-rainbow-body/). Among those who have attempted a study of this phenomenon are the Carthusian Brother David Steindl-Rast, who has collaborated with a Roman Catholic priest, Francis Tiso, a scholar deeply versed in Tibetan culture; for more, see Gail Holland l (March–May 2002). "Christian Buddhist Explorations: The Rainbow Body," *Institute of Noetic Sciences Review* 59 (March–May 2002). F. Tiso, *Rainbow Body and Resurrection: Spiritual Attainment, the Dissolution of the Material Body, and the Case of Khenpo A Chö* (San Francisco: North Atlantic Books, 2016). An American holistic practitioner, Dr. Asa Hershoff, offers a fine scientific overview, "Rainbow Body 1: Science Meets Light" on the webpage: https://www.drasahershoff.com/science-meet-the-rainbow-body/.

80. Stewart, *Evolution's Arrow*, 42, 45. This cooperative strain is certainly a major feature of our existence as a human species, an endowment overshadowed, and even undermined, by the ferocious competition that characterizes our contemporary world and bolstered by several of the leading advocates of Darwinian evolution. I consider cooperation to be a central feature of our species, individually and collectively, as does the Dutch social historian Rutger Bregman (2020). The claim must always be considered, however, within the paradoxical nature of universal life as outlined in chapter four above. This paradoxical element is vividly portrayed by the Malasyian scientist Ed Yong (2016) in his fascinating rendition of our microbial and bacterial world. While cooperation is a major feature, he provides several examples of competition as well, even at times highly destructive; paradox prevails at every level of our being and becoming. Also worth remembering here is the Judaeo-Christian command: Love God as you love your neighbor, and love your neighbor as you love yourself (Mark 12:30–31). Authentic love of the other is not possible without a prior propensity for self-love. It almost sounds like selfishness is a precondition for relational selfhood—paradox at work once again.

81. Standard physics knows well what we mean by field influence, You will get valuable and relevant information from Levy (2018), Winter (2009), and Schafer (2013). To appreciate the experiential significance of such fields and how they relate to human life, however, I suggest you consult experienced healers, and they will enlighten you better than any written source.

82. Palmer, *Gravity and Grace*, 180.

Afterword: Paradox and Synodality

83. Several Catholic sources claim that the vocations' crisis is a Western problem, not a universal one. In fact, every country in Central and South America has seen a decline in vocations over the past twenty years. Also, some African countries such as South Africa. Moreover, in countries where there is still a large intake, there is also a steady stream of departures (even after ordination), a dimension scarcely never reported.

84. Kubler-Ross, *On Death and Dying.*

85. Vearncombe et al., *After Jesus, Before Christianity.*

86. Delio, *Making All Things New.*

ACKNOWLEDGMENTS

Looking back on my life story, I owe a debt of gratitude to the various "families" around and within whom this autobiography is woven. My blood family continues to provide friendship and bioregional grounding that renews and revitalizes my living spirit, a simple but persistent reminder of what unconditional love is all about.

My religious family of the Missionaries of the Sacred Heart generously and graciously affirmed my missionary outreach, not merely in my home country of Ireland, but also in the Philippines, Australia, and the USA. That heart-felt solidarity is a gift I deeply cherish.

In the short few years of my early religious formation in the Milltown Institute of Dublin, Ireland, I was introduced to another kind of family that extended over many years as I used the Institute's library for ongoing research. To all the library staff, I owe a deep debt of gratitude.

The fruit of that research took a quantum leap when Mike Leach, then managing director at Crossroad publications, began publishing my books and continued to do so when he moved to Orbis, Maryknoll. What an amazing inspiring and challenging family Orbis has been to me, thanks to Mike Leach, Robert Ellsberg, and all who work there.

I lived in the UK for over thirty years, working and living with a range of people, many of whom have become life-long friends. Indeed, it was through that more amorphous kind of family that I first experienced what the Gospel notion of the companionship of empowerment really means.

About twenty years ago, I began exploring the landscape of Adult Faith Development, an exploration that continues alongside a vast family, lay and religious, across several countries.

Too many to name individually, I owe these people—and particularly the wise elders among them—my deepest gratitude for opening up with me horizons of faith so full of hope and promise.

Finally, with the publication of this book, I am encountering a branch of the Franciscan family, whose charism has inspired me over many years. I am grateful to the publishing team I am working with and particularly Diane M. Houdek, OFS, whose wisdom and editorial skill has brought this book to birth, moulding it into a narrative which I hope every reader will enjoy.